Pauline Hopkins and the American Dream

An African American Writer's (Re)Visionary Gospel of Success

Alisha R. Knight

The University of Tennessee Press / Knoxville

An earlier version of chapter 2 appeared as "Furnace Blasts for the Tuskegee Wizard" in *American Periodicals* 17.1 (2007): 41–64, published by The Ohio State University Press. It is used here with the permission of the publisher.

An earlier version of chapter 4 appeared as "'All Things Work Together for Good': Pauline Hopkins's Race Woman and the Gospel of Success" in *Loopholes and Retreats: African American Writers and the Nineteenth Century*, edited by John Cullen Gruesser and Hanna Wallinger (Vienna: Lit Verlag, 2009), 125–40. It is used here with the permission of the publisher.

The paper in this book meets the requirements of American National Standards Institute / National Information Standards Organization specification Z39.48-1992 (Permanence of Paper). It contains 30 percent post-consumer waste and is certified by the Forest Stewardship Council.

Library of Congress Cataloging-in-Publication Data

Knight, Alisha R.
Pauline Hopkins and the American dream: an African American writer's (re)visionary gospel of success / Alisha R. Knight. — 1st ed.
        p. cm.
Includes bibliographical references and index.
ISBN-13: 978-1-57233-852-4 (hardcover)
ISBN-10: 1-57233-852-0 (hardcover)
1. Hopkins, Pauline E. (Pauline Elizabeth)—Criticism and interpretation.
2. American fiction—African American authors—History and criticism.
3. American fiction—Women authors—History and criticism.
4. African American women authors—Intellectual life.
I. Title.

PS1999.H4226Z73 2012
818'.409—dc22   2011041682

CONTENTS

ILLUSTRATIONS

Acknowledgments

This book was long in the making, and I want to express my gratitude to the Woodrow Wilson National Fellowship Foundation for awarding me a Career Enhancement Fellowship, and to Washington College for providing me support through its faculty enhancement grants and Christian A. Johnson Fellowship junior faculty leave program. I would not have been able to complete this book without the financial support and release from my teaching and service responsibilities that I received from these institutions. The Interlibrary Loan staff at Drew University and Washington College worked their magic to help me secure materials that were difficult to find. I am especially grateful to Beth M. Howse, the special collections librarian at Fisk University, for her assistance and for providing me with a copy of Hopkins's correspondence with William Monroe Trotter and John Freund. I would like to express my sincere appreciation to Scot Danforth, Kerry Webb, and the editorial staff at the University of Tennessee Press for recognizing this book's potential and for their guidance throughout this publishing process.

I would also like to thank a number of colleagues, mentors, and friends, namely Tanya Clark, Ira Dworkin, John Gruesser, the late Merrill Skaggs, Geraldine Smith-Wright, Susan Vowels, Hanna Wallinger, and Traci West, who have read versions of this manuscript and shared their valuable insight with me. My family, the Colemans and the Knights, have provided unwavering support throughout this process. My sister, Marilyn Coleman, deserves special recognition for her keen eye. My husband, Vincent, also did his part by lovingly and repeatedly reminding me that I needed to finish this book.

INTRODUCTION

In 1904, Pauline Elizabeth Hopkins wrote an article describing the technological advancements of the New York City subway system for *The Voice of the Negro*. Interestingly, at the end of the article, Hopkins cautioned readers not to rest on their laurels. Even though the rapid transit system was a significant accomplishment for a city equated with "the road to success," Hopkins made a point of admonishing that "we hope that the warning words of Emerson will forever impress this country and its citizens: 'The civility of no race is perfect whilst another race is degraded.'"[1] In essence, Hopkins used this article to argue that upper- and middle-class Anglo Americans could not boast of their cultural refinement and moral superiority, as evidenced in these technological advancements, as long as racism continued to subjugate African Americans. According to historian Nell Irvin Painter, during the last decades of the nineteenth century, "Americans endowed technology with qualities they imagined to be uniquely American: prosperity, mobility, and democracy."[2] For Hopkins, true American democracy and the civility of its entire citizenry could be achieved only when people of color were no longer prevented from contributing to, and fully benefiting from, the nation's prosperity. Indeed, Hopkins's concern for the progress and success of the American people, especially of African Americans, was not isolated to the subject of this single article; rather, it occupied her literary imagination throughout her career. Through journalism, drama, short stories, and novels, Hopkins endeavored to expose the racism and sexism inherent in both the gospel of success and the iconic image of the self-made man.

The self-made man is a common trope in late-nineteenth- and early twentieth-century popular American literature and culture. The working and middle classes faced significant challenges during the Gilded Age, from labor disputes to economic depressions. Both children and adults sought what Paulette Kilmer calls "a refuge from modernity" by reading archetypal tales of poor young boys working to become successful businessmen.[3] It is important to note that the gospel of success did not embody the reality of American society at the turn of the twentieth century. In actuality, few working- and middle-class people were able to follow the tenets of the gospel of success and achieve wealth, regardless of their ethnicity. Kilmer observes that, "real workers frequently rose to supervisory positions, while fewer than ten in every one hundred millionaires had grown up in lower-class families."[4] Furthermore, scholars have noted the definition of success has varied over time. For example, there is a significant difference in opinion about the importance of wealth in the success formula and the historical periods when it has been most crucial. Richard Huber claims that "In America, success has meant making money and translating it into status, or becoming famous."[5] For Huber it has also meant "attaining riches or achieving fame."[6] Yet, Richard Weiss cautions that "in current parlance, 'wealth' and 'success' are used as synonyms; this was not so through much of the nineteenth century."[7] Rex Burns concurs that success has not always denoted wealth: "indeed, it was not until the mid-nineteenth century that such a definition became a sanctioned code."[8] These varied emphases on wealth do not belie the fact that success necessitated moderate to high earnings or net worth. Still, there is a consensus that the self-made man of this period achieved some form of affluence, eminence, respectability, and social mobility, while personal virtues of the self-made man included "Thrift, perseverance, loyalty, integrity, [and] honor."[9] Very few literary critics address the role that the self-made man and success literature played in the lives of turn-of-the-century African Americans; however, Hopkins believed such literature served the African American community in ways that did more than offer readers an escape from the real world. For Hopkins, fiction was "a record of growth and development from generation to generation" and she believed she could use popular literature—fiction and nonfiction—to encourage and track the black community's progress.[10]

Ever since Pauline Hopkins's work was rediscovered in the mid-twentieth century, literary scholars have focused their efforts on situating her within the sentimental and domestic literary traditions of nineteenth-century women's writing. In Ann Allen Shockley's 1972 watershed article, "Pauline Elizabeth Hopkins: A Biographical Excursion Into Obscurity," she notes that the depiction of mob violence and lynching contained in Contending Forces "is told in the genteel and romantic fashion typical of its time."[11] Identifying sentimental forms in turn-of-the-century fiction has become a mainstay of literary criticism, and scholars habitually constrict discussions of Hopkins's work to this literary genre. In "Pauline Hopkins: Our Literary Foremother," Claudia Tate advocates for an increase in scholarly attention toward Hopkins by highlighting how "in being both black and female, she documents the cross section of the literary concerns of two major groups of American writers: turn-of-the-century black writers, who primarily dramatized themes of racial injustice, and mid- to late-nineteenth-century white women writers, some of whom wrote sentimental and domestic novels that acclaimed Christian virtue."[12] According to Kate McCullough, "literary critics agree that the post-Reconstruction fiction of African American women such as Hopkins and Frances E. W. Harper reflects a desire to 'uplift' the race by offering self-representations that refuted the multiple received stereotypes of African American women. Critics have also agreed that to this end these authors use the vehicle of the sentimental novel, producing heroines who celebrate domesticity, marriage, and motherhood, and who reflect a dominant white model of virtuous womanhood."[13]

Some critics have noticed that certain components of her work, like the figure of the self-made man, do not fit within the sentimental tradition. Instead of exploring the significance of this, they have dismissed these components and criticized her for assimilating white middle-class values. For example, during the tail end of the Black Arts movement, Gwendolyn Brooks misinterpreted Hopkins's objective for treating the figure of the self-made man in her fiction, and argued *Contending Forces* has "assimilationist urges."[14] By assuming that Hopkins's interest "was *not* in Revolution *nor* exhaustive Revision," Brooks seemed disappointed that Hopkins was not overtly "radical" like Richard Wright, Ralph Ellison, or Margaret Walker: "Often doth the brainwashed slave revere the modes and idolatries of the master. And Pauline Hopkins consistently proves herself a continuing slave, despite little bursts of righteous heat."[15] Mary Helen Washington followed Brooks's lead in *Invented Lives*, arguing that Hopkins was less militant than Frances E. W. Harper and "less able to express her anger toward whites." She asked, "with such freedom to speak directly to a sympathetic black audience, why is Hopkins still a prisoner to an ideology that ultimately supports white superiority?"[16] The editors of *Twentieth-Century Literary Criticism* provided another misreading of Hopkins in their assessment that "throughout her career Hopkins protested the inequities suffered by her race, advocating assimilation and integration with the white community as a remedy to racial injustice."[17] Yet a closer look at Hopkins's fiction and nonfiction reveals she produced a body of literature that does in fact perform, to use Brooks's term, an "exhaustive Revision" of, and even debunks, the ever-popular idea of the "American Dream."

Hopkins began her professional writing career when blacks began losing the optimism they experienced during the Reconstruction period. Though the Civil War brought an end to slavery, it introduced a myriad of questions about the status of black people, particularly newly freed slaves, in

United States society. Debates about voting rights and the control of black labor continued to divide sections of the nation. According to Eric Foner, "Lurking behind these debates was a broader question suggested by the end of slavery: Should the freedmen be viewed as ready to take their place as citizens and participants in the competitive marketplace, or did their unique historical experience oblige the federal government to take special action on their behalf?"[18] With the establishment of the Freedmen's Bureau in 1865, it appeared that federal intervention was a requisite for African American economic and political survival. With the ratification of the Thirteenth, Fourteenth, and Fifteenth Amendments, and as blacks were elected to local, state, and national offices, the African American community experienced a brief period of optimism about its ability to achieve equal rights in the United States. But a number of events in the late 1870s, including the Democratic "redemption" of Congress in 1875 and the overturning of the Civil Rights Act in 1877, signaled the end of this optimism. Influential blacks turned to institutions within the African American community, like churches, schools, and small businesses, to achieve localized prominence, influence, and financial success. As Foner notes, for blacks who were "Severed from any larger political purpose, economic self-help, especially among the emerging black middle class, became an alternative to involvement in public life. . . . In general, black activity turned inward. Assuming a defensive cast, it concentrated on strengthening the black community rather than on directly challenging the new status quo."[19] In light of the discordant social, economic, and political climate of the United States during the turn of the century, it seems only fitting that Hopkins chose to use her work to expose the limits of the traditional success formula. In this sense she was like her black contemporaries who wrote African American literature that "was used to confirm and to manifest creativity and genius while also documenting and shaping social, political, and spiritual aspirations and conditions."[20]

Still, Hopkins's treatment of the success archetype set her apart from many of her peers for its consistency in criticizing United States policy toward blacks and promoting agitation rather than integration. Hopkins's writing responded to white oppression by criticizing and revising the success myth and also by offering African Americans an alternative model for success that embraces African American culture. Whereas some of her contemporaries, like Booker T. Washington and Alice Moore Dunbar-Nelson, limited their commentary on success to their nonfiction or just a handful of texts, Hopkins employed and revised the theme not only in her dramatic, fictional, and nonfictional work, but also in the editorial decisions she made as a member of the *Colored American Magazine* staff. Furthermore, it is because of the great extent to which Hopkins employed the success literary genre that we should consider it more instrumental than any other genre, including and especially the sentimental novel, to Hopkins's project. No other genre fostered discourses about the possibilities or lack of opportunities for African Americans as readily as success literature, and Hopkins was the first African American woman to write extensively in this genre.

Henry Louis Gates's African American literary theory of "Signification," the "repetition of formal structures and their difference," provides a useful theoretical framework for exploring how Hopkins debunks the gospel of success and revises the trope of the self-made man.[21] According to Gates, "Writers Signify upon each other's texts by rewriting the received textual tradition. This can be accomplished by the revision of tropes. This sort of Signifyin(g) revision serves, if successful, to create a space for the revising text. . . . The revising text is written in the language of the tradition, employing its tropes, its rhetorical strategies, and its ostensible subject matter."[22] In this regard, the traditional gospel of success served as the "formal structure" that Hopkins repeated and altered. Hopkins subscribed to the concepts of affluence, eminence, and social mobility, but she revised the definition of success by expanding the meaning of social respectability to include freedom from racial discrimination. She repeated this formal structure in her drama, short stories, and novels yet, at the same time, she Signified[23] on this model by showing how the formal structure prohibited the traditional self-made man from existing in the African American community and being fully recognized by mainstream white culture. In this sense, by stating that Hopkins either Signified on or revised the traditional model, I am arguing that she adapted or altered the traditional archetype, without completely overturning it, for the purpose of correcting or improving it.

Hopkins's own life can be read as one black woman's attempt to become successful and self-made. Two Hopkins biographies, Hanna Wallinger's *Pauline E. Hopkins: A Literary Biography* and Lois Brown's *Pauline Elizabeth Hopkins: Black Daughter of the Revolution*, make reciting Hopkins's full life story unnecessary. However, a few details related to her literary endeavors are worth highlighting here. Hopkins was born in Portland, Maine, in 1859 to Northrup Hopkins and Sarah Allen. Her writing career began during her adolescence in Boston; at age fifteen her essay, "The Evils of Intemperance and Their Remedy," won a contest sponsored by The Congregational Publishing Society of Boston and William Wells Brown. As a young adult, Hopkins pursued a number of professions, including singing, acting, and stenography. Theater programs in Hopkins's scrapbook show that her drama career spanned almost a decade, from 1877 to 1885. Her first dramatic performance was as "Pauline Western, the Belle of Saratoga" in March 1877, when at age eighteen she performed under the stage name Pauline E.

MISS PAULINE E. HOPKINS

PROF. SILAS X. FLOYD

Miss Pauline E. Hopkins was at one time the leading writer for the Colored American Magazine of Boston. She has consented to be one of our regular contributors for 1905. She will open up in February in her first of a series of articles on "The Dark Races of the Twentieth Century." This series of articles will compose a historical regime of the history, habits, customs and locations of the several dark races now brought prominently before the world as "perils" to civilization, and will in themselves be well worth a year's subscription to the magazine. Miss Hopkins will also contribute a few short stories during the year.

Silas X. Floyd will continue to edit "Wayside." This has become one of the most popular departments of our magazine, and will be more interesting than ever.

In addition to these we have engaged articles from President A. P. Camphor of the College of the West Coast of Africa, Hon. Edward Wilmot Blyden, of Liberia, Hon. Archibald Grimke, of Boston, Hon. Daniel Murray, Mrs. Fannie Barrier Williams, Miss Nannie H. Burroughs, and many others.

In our Monthly Review we will cover the leading events of the month, and "In the Sanctum" we shall discuss many problems of the day.

HON. ARCHIBALD H. GRIMKE

MRS. FANNIE B. WILLIAMS

MISS NANNIE H. BURROUGHS

People who want to keep well informed ought to read our magazine. Subscription price one dollar per year. Ten cents per copy.

THE VOICE OF THE NEGRO,

913 Austell Building, Atlanta, Ga.

Pauline Hopkins. From the December 1904 issue of Voice of the Negro.

Allen.[24] According to Eileen Southern, Hopkins copyrighted her first musical, *Aristocracy*, in August 1877.[25] She also completed another play, *Winona*, in 1878.[26] Unfortunately, no text of the theatrical production of *Winona* or *Aristocracy* has been found. Hopkins's next play, *Peculiar Sam; or, The Underground Railroad* (1879), was originally performed by Z. W. Sprague's Original Georgia Minstrels.[27] Later, it was performed by her family's theater group, the Hopkins Colored Troubadours, with Sam Lucas and the Hyers Sisters in Boston in 1880. The play received good reviews, and throughout the early 1880s Hopkins was known as "Boston's Favorite Colored Soprano."[28] Aside from her dramatic career, Hopkins's most productive literary period was from 1900 to 1904 when she published four novels, at least seven short stories, and numerous nonfiction magazine articles while editing the *Colored American Magazine*.

Hopkins was a dedicated editor and contributor to the *Colored American Magazine*. In 1904 she helped found the Colored American League and worked to increase subscriptions and raise funding for the magazine. According to Shockley, the magazine's circulation grew to 15,000 while Hopkins was its editor.[29] Hopkins left the magazine in late 1904 after it was purchased by Booker T. Washington. She continued her writing career by contributing her "New York Subway" article and a series on "The Dark Races of the Twentieth Century" to the *Voice of the Negro* in 1904 and 1905, respectively. In 1905 she founded her own publishing firm, Pauline E. Hopkins and Company, and published *A Primer of Facts Pertaining to the Early Greatness of the African Race and the Possibility of Restoration by Its Descendants, with Epilogue*. In 1916 she became the editor of another periodical, *New Era Magazine*, which lasted only two issues. After this magazine failed, Hopkins retreated from public life and resumed her work as a stenographer. It appears that by the time Hopkins died on August 13, 1930, her important work as an editor and writer had long been forgotten.

According to Richard Yarborough, Hopkins was "the single most productive black woman writer at the turn of the century."[30] Yet, for most of the twentieth century she had been considered a minor literary figure, and it has taken some time for the critical reception of Hopkins's writing to evolve from cursory dismissals to serious considerations of her multifaceted contributions to African American literary history. The bulk of the early criticism, from the 1930s to the 1970s, focused on *Contending Forces*. Vernon Loggins criticized the novel for being over-sensationalized, and Hugh Gloster characterized it as being "over plotted."[31] Robert Bone offered hardly any justification for categorizing Hopkins as an "accommodationist."[32] Hopkins's work began to receive more attention in the 1970s because of Ann Allen Shockley's aforementioned article, "Pauline Elizabeth Hopkins: A

Biographical Excursion Into Obscurity," which was one of the first substantial biographical pieces. Two chapters from *Contending Forces*, "Friendship" and "The Sewing Circle," along with Hopkins's short story, "Bro'r Abr'm Jimson's Wedding," were anthologized in Mary Helen Washington's *Invented Lives* as an example of black women's writing that was being "rediscovered and reevaluated by feminist critics" in the mid-1980s.[33]

Hazel Carby helped redirect our attention to Hopkins's popular fiction and editorial work at the *Colored American Magazine*. In *Reconstructing Womanhood* Carby argued that "any attempt to gain a comprehensive understanding of her fiction must begin with an analysis of all her work for the *Colored American Magazine*.[34] Carby was among the first to examine Hopkins's serialized novels, noting how she incorporated "strategies and formulas of the sensational fiction of dime novels and magazines," namely "the elements of suspense, action, adventure, complex plotting, multiple and false identities, and the use of disguise" to "create stories of political and social critique."[35] The Schomburg library of Nineteenth Century Black Women Writers reprinted *Contending Forces* and Hopkins's three serialized novels, *Hagar's Daughter, Winona*, and *Of One Blood*, in 1988. In the introduction, once again Carby called attention to Hopkins's use of popular fiction to reveal "the limits of these popular American narrative forms for black characterization."[36] Interestingly, in both her monograph and introduction to the Schomburg volume, Carby omitted the success novel from the list of popular literary forms that Hopkins critiqued or produced herself. In Yarborough's introduction to the Schomburg edition of *Contending Forces*, he recognized Hopkins's racial uplift project that entailed "presenting Afro-American readers with moral guidance and instruction through exemplary characters"; yet, he also pointed to the "sentimental romance" as the genre Hopkins used to counteract black stereotypes and depict black characters "who would be acknowledged by the white reader not only as human beings but also as embodiments of white bourgeois values, manners, and tastes."[37]

Claudia Tate's *Domestic Allegories of Political Desire* explored Hopkins's use of "popular formulaic plot lines of the detective story, the western, and the psychological ghost story to repudiate the resurgence of racial prejudice and discrimination during the post-Reconstruction period."[38] The publication of *The Unruly Voice: Rediscovering Pauline Elizabeth Hopkins*, a collection of critical essays, signaled a renewed interest in her work. Most recently, Ira Dworkin has edited a collection of Hopkins's *Colored American Magazine* nonfiction. Still, despite efforts to reconsider the relevance of popular literary forms to Hopkins's work, literary scholars continue to overlook the relevance of success literature and the purposes to which Hopkins used it. Understanding how the success literature figures in Hopkins's oeuvre is bound to result in a more comprehensive understanding of her visionary mission and her revisionist writings.

This "whole author study," to borrow Yarborough's term, of Hopkins's published novels, short stories, essays, and drama examines how she used the theme of racial uplift, the pursuit of social progress, and the figure of the self-made man to propound her theories and to demonstrate the limitations of the traditional success model. Her writings show how an ideal already unrealistic for a majority of working- and middle-class whites is even less germane to the African American experience. In addition to revealing the inadequacies of the traditional success model, Hopkins offered a revised model that emphasizes not only the achievement of social respectability and freedom from racial discrimination, but the attainment of these things in a community where blacks work together to support each other while they pursue equal rights. This element of "racial uplift" is key to Hopkins's radical revision of the traditional success paradigm. Chapter 1 provides a historical overview of the self-made man and defines the success archetype. I rely on key scholars in this field, including John G. Cawelti, Richard Huber, Paulette Kilmer, and Richard Weiss to establish the formal paradigm of American success, then I provide further insight into Hopkins's intellectual and political thought in relation to her contemporaries. This chapter also establishes her definition of success by using the nonfiction articles she wrote for the *Colored American Magazine* and *New Era Magazine*, such as "Charles Winter Wood: From Bootblack to Professor," and her series "Famous Men of the Negro Race" and "Men of Vision." As part of her critique of the American Dream, Hopkins took the iconic Booker T. Washington to task in her characterization of him in *Contending Forces*, and her critique of his policies in her nonfiction journalism provides an opportunity to understand the broad scope of her project. Chapter 2 discusses the various tactics Hopkins used to expose the limits of Washington's self-help program and explores her conflicts with his supporters, which culminated in her dismissal from the *Colored American Magazine* after he purchased it. This chapter also considers Hopkins in relation to another contemporary black intellectual, W. E. B. Du Bois. Chapter 3 discusses how Hopkins repeated the trope of the self-made man, "with a difference," in her drama and fiction to Signify on the traditional success model and define her own more appropriate success model for the black community. I use characters from nineteenth-century popular novels by Horatio Alger to illustrate how *Peculiar Sam, Contending Forces,* and *Of One Blood* Signify on the traditional white success model. Though Alger is among the scores of popular authors of the period, like William Taylor Adams (Oliver Optic), who wrote about the gospel of success, I have chosen to single out his works because they are considered the most popular and representative of the period. The definition of success and the American Dream were applied to men and women differently. Men were typically tested and rewarded outside the home, while women were circumscribed to private, domestic spaces and were taught to value and assess their progress and success accordingly. Chapter 4 considers the extent to which definitions of success differed for black men and black women and it examines the extent to which Hopkins revised the success archetype for black women. Hopkins's ideology about women and success was influenced by representations of the Gibson Girl, the New Woman, and the New Negro Woman. In *Contending Forces, Hagar's Daughter,* and *Winona,* Hopkins illustrated how racialized sexual exploitation made it almost impossible for black women to succeed solely by their own efforts.

CHAPTER 1

"To Aid in Everyway Possible in Uplifting the Colored People of America": Hopkins's Revisionary Definition of African American Success

During the late nineteenth and early twentieth centuries, the phrase "self-made man" invoked the image of an autonomous male who became wealthy and powerful through his ambition, hard work, and shrewd judgment. According to Richard Weiss, "Tradition has it that every American child receives, as part of his birthright, the freedom to mold his own life. . . . The belief that all men, in accordance with certain rules, but exclusively by their own efforts, can make of their lives what they will has been widely popularized for well over a century."[1] This tradition, generally referred to as the "American Dream" or the "gospel of success," has deep roots in American culture, and there is an entire body of what I call "success literature"—self-improvement guides, biographical dictionaries, autobiographical narratives, and novels—that prescribes and perpetuates this belief system. The figure of the self-made man is a common trope in fictional and nonfictional "rags-to-riches" or, more accurately, "rags-to-respectability" narratives, where a young hero moves from the country to the city, or from the gutter to the penthouse, searching for employment opportunities and a better quality of life. Once he secures entry-level employment, he incrementally works his way up through the ranks from a menial laborer to become an office manager, corporate executive, or entrepreneur.

Although success literature and the self-made man are not unique to American culture, the origins of the American rendering of the gospel of success have been traced back to Puritan advice guides that instructed early settlers how to conduct themselves in a proper Christian manner. For example, in *A Christian at His Calling* (1701), the Puritan minister Cotton Mather explains to readers that they have "a General Calling, which is, to Serve the Lord Jesus Christ, and Save his own Soul, in the Services of *Religion*," and "a Personal Calling; or a certain *Particular Employment*, by which his *Usefulness*, in his Neighborhood, is distinguished."[2] Puritans believed that everyone's personal calling should service and help others, should not be sinful, and should be compatible with his personality. A Christian should perform his job well and not be "Slothful in Business."[3] He should conduct his business affairs with diligence, discretion, honesty, contentment, and piety. Pursuing this personal calling should not be done at the expense of the general calling; hence, Christians were instructed to pray every day and not to conduct business on Sunday. From this type of advice grew the Protestant work ethic in which success was tied to religious duty and dutiful Christians sought material success in the name of God. Rex Burns observes that it was important to be fruitful, but "the fruitful *use* of wealth—great or small—was far more important in judging a person than was the mere possession of wealth."[4] Thus, to justify the immense wealth accumulated by some individuals while others remained poor, successful men were expected to be Christian stewards and perform charitable works to help the less fortunate members of society. Another religious justification for wealth was that "the man who was not free to be fruitful was not free to worship through action."[5] Puritan success was not expected to result in great wealth, per se, but in a moderate income that enabled economic independence and social respectability. It was not until the mid-nineteenth century that great wealth was associated with success. "Before that," according to Burns, "beginning with Puritans and modified by the Enlightenment, success was most often associated with a figure of middling income who worked his own fee-simple farm, the yeoman."[6]

By the late 1700s, the gospel of success became increasingly secular, and the successful man began to cultivate virtues that were more ethical than moral. Benjamin Franklin is often considered the archetype of the self-made man in the United States. One of Franklin's most popular texts, *The Way to Wealth*, links seventeenth- and eighteenth-century assumptions about the meaning of success and how to achieve it. *The Way to Wealth* promotes the virtues of industry and frugality and discourages idleness and extravagance. It includes practical quotations of Franklin's Poor Richard persona, including: "God helps them that help themselves," "Sloth makes all things difficult, but industry all easy," "Early to bed, and early to rise, makes a man healthy, wealthy, and wise," and "Diligence is the mother of good luck, and God gives all things to industry."[7] Weiss notes that whereas Puritans (like Mather) believed that men were born into fixed social spheres and that trying to move above one's station was considered a sinful ambition, "Franklin, on the other hand, encouraged the wish to advance in the social hierarchy."[8] Another difference between Mather and Franklin, according to Richard Huber, is that Mather believed acquiring wealth was a way of worshiping God; Franklin's goals were more earthbound: "what Franklin did was to preserve the means and immediate goal of wealth of Puritanism, but then went on to diminish its theological sanction by emphasizing a utilitarian justification. . . . Benevolence, then, was to be done in the name of a secular humanitarianism with man as the final purpose, not the ritual faith in God."[9] Thus, whereas Mather believed in tithing 10 percent of one's wealth for God, Franklin was not as dogmatic.

In the mid- to late-nineteenth century both religious and secular justifications for the accumulation of wealth and success prevailed. In fact, according to John Cawelti, there were at least two major strains of the success formula prevalent in popular literature during the Gilded Age. One was an older, "Conservative-Protestant Tradition" where success equaled the "attainment of a respectable competence in this world and eternal salvation in the world to come." The other, newer strain maintained an economic emphasis that was often mixed with the Protestant ethic and held the values of "initiative, aggressiveness, competitiveness and forcefulness."[10] As time progressed, writers who produced success literature continued to justify acquiring wealth as a means of helping others, and readers were reminded that wealth was not an end in itself. Yet, by the end of the nineteenth century, "the dominant concept of success was one of opulent materialism competitively won."[11] The original, religious ideal did not become completely obsolete, however. The rapid geographical expansion and technological changes of the period created a sense of conflict between economic advancement and traditional social and religious mores. As a result, American culture experienced some anxiety and felt uncertain about the meaning of individuals' lives and personal moral duties. Hence many Americans clung to the religious prescription for success.

Sketches of poor young boys striving to become successful businessmen were read by working- and middle-class adults and children not only for inspiration to better themselves, but also to escape the realities of economic hardship. Indeed, the American success myth and the trope of the self-made man served dual purposes in late nineteenth- and early twentieth-century society. On the one hand, they provided models for working- and middle-class citizens to aspire to. Although post–Civil War technological advancements like the telegraph and the transcontinental railroad contributed to the rapid development of the nation's major cities and to a shift from an agrarian to an industrial economy and culture, as Paulette Kilmer notes, "frequently, progress intensified the misery of the poor, even while raising their standard of living."[12] Even though new industrial centers offered job opportunities, labor conditions were often hard. The growing steel industry, for example, was "the showpiece of American progress," Nell Painter explains; yet, "labor conditions in the steel industry were exceedingly harsh. For less than subsistence wages, workers put in twelve-hour days and seven-day weeks."[13] Furthermore, in 1900, "between 60 and 88 percent of Americans were poor or very poor."[14] Not only were the workdays long and the salaries low, but hazardous work environments were commonplace. Violent labor disputes and strikes increased during the decades at the close of the nineteenth and beginning of the twentieth centuries. In light of the limited opportunities for advancement that many workers faced, biographical sketches of self-made men in popular magazines offered audiences real-life examples of men who rose from humble beginnings to earn respectable positions with increased wealth. On the other hand, the success myth also served to placate these same working- and middle-class individuals who were struggling in a capitalist society. Weiss has argued that in popular literature for the masses, "the 'rags-to-riches' tradition, by creating an illusion of opportunity, served as a social pacifier inimical to reform."[15] Thus, stories about self-made men offered readers an escape from their humdrum existences. "In fantasy," Kilmer explains, the working and middle classes "briefly attained the success that often eluded them in the real world."[16]

Some self-improvement literature during this period distinguished between materialism and success and "sought above all to strike a balance between traditional social and religious ideals and the spirit of individual economic enterprise."[17] For example, in *The Art of Money-Getting* (1882), circus businessman P. T. Barnum advises his readers, "To get rich, is not always equivalent to being successful. 'There are many rich poor men,' while there are many others, honest and devout men and women, who have never possessed so much money as some rich persons squander in a week, but who are nevertheless really richer and happier than any man can ever be while he is a transgressor of the higher laws of his being."[18] Such literature advocated patience and manual labor and deplored the speed at which new millionaires were being made. Instead, people were encouraged to aspire to a profession that would make them comfortable and not rich, because everyone could not become a captain of industry.[19]

Actually, the assertion that all Americans could not become captains of industry is an understatement. The political and economic realities of the time indicate that blacks had fewer opportunities to become wealthy than any other group. History has shown that blacks were more severely affected by segregation than other ethnic American populations. Jim Crow laws that legally mandated that blacks and whites travel in separate train cars, drink out of separate water fountains, attend separate schools, and live in separate neighborhoods, for example, did not formally apply to Asian Americans, Mexican Americans, or Jewish Americans. John Sibley Butler's study of black entrepreneurship explains how segregation kept blacks from the open market and restricted their business enterprises in ways that did not affect other ethnic groups. "Although there was conflict based on ethnicity," Butler argues, "there were never explicit ethnic programs developed by state governments to control their every movements [sic]. This governmental control took away the opportunity for Afro-American business to compete in a truly open market. This is one of the fundamental differences between Afro-American business and ethnic American business."[20]

Success literature at the turn of the twentieth century assumed the guise of popular literature that targeted a broad, mass reading audience whose education and reading tastes varied but would not be considered erudite. A number of scholars have assumed that no one produced any popular literature, and by extension, success literature, specifically for turn-of-the-century black readers. For example, Weiss has observed that mainstream success literature targeted native-born, Protestant, middle-class whites and that there was a "nativist bias" in these texts.[21] Yet, other sources indicate the black working- and middle-class communities were just as hungry for success literature as whites, perhaps even more so. For example, Michael Fultz's article, "'The Morning Cometh': African American Periodicals, Education, and the Black Middle Class, 1900–1930," discusses how several early twentieth-century black journals, such as the *Colored American Magazine, The Voice of the Negro,* and *Alexander's Magazine,* addressed black higher education. Referring to members of the emerging black middle class, Fultz explains that "Among other traits, they were decidedly race conscious, and they forcefully advocated self-help, character-building, social uplift, and race patronage and solidarity."[22] They read black journals that "were established to demonstrate the race's capabilities and to disseminate the African-American point of view." Furthermore, the emphasis on black higher education in these journals "powerfully illuminated a distinct meaning of progress and helped to define a vision of social uplift."[23] African Americans were an ideal audience for success literature because of their intense desire to rise up and overcome racial segregation and discrimination. August Meier's *Negro Thought in America, 1880–1915,* discusses the specific requirements for progress in the black middle class: "thrift, industry, frugality, morality, land ownership and the acquisition of wealth."[24] Meier traces these values back to the Reconstruction period, when blacks "focused their attention upon becoming full-fledged citizens. The franchise, education, guarantees for civil rights, the acquisition of property and wealth, and the cultivation of morality were all designed to elevate Negroes and achieve their integration into American society."[25] Post-Reconstruction black leaders believed economic success achieved through racial solidarity and self-help would earn the black masses the respect of whites and the full benefits of United States citizenship. This belief "was based upon the assumption that by the acquisition of wealth and morality—attained largely by their own efforts—Negroes would gain the respect of white men and thus be accorded their rights as citizens."[26] In short, the American gospel of success was as much a part of the black cultural ethos as it was of white culture. After Reconstruction, blacks increasingly viewed wealth as a sign of success and they adopted "the ideas of the gospel of wealth and Social Darwinism and applied them to their own racial situation."[27]

African Americans have a history of producing and reading success literature, either in the form of autobiographical narratives or biographical dictionaries and collected sketches of prominent individuals. One can readily identify African American texts that manifest the black community's preoccupation with both individual success and race progress, although twenty-first-century readers might not typically use the term "self-help" or "success literature" when referring to these works. Slave narratives, for example, which served to advocate the abolition of slavery, not only established the black author's humanity but also contributed to the discourse on the American Dream. James Olney's study of the slave narrative's literary conventions has made it clear that slave narratives possessed "very specific motives, intentions, and uses," which were "to reveal the truth of slavery and so to bring about its abolition."[28] But the literary conventions that we are accustomed to identifying with the slave narrative can also be mapped to the typical success narrative. For example, when Frederick Douglass provides a limited account of his parentage in *Narrative of the Life of Frederick Douglass* (1845), and when he describes the plantation system in which he and other enslaved blacks were deprived of adequate food and clothing and were subjected to dehumanizing physical abuse, he establishes himself as the lone hero determined to overcome his "humble beginnings" to achieve not only freedom, but also dignity and respectability. Douglass's observations of freedom in the North provide opportunities for him to comment on the gospel of success. When he recounts his impressions of New Bedford, Massachusetts, upon his arrival, he describes signs of a community that is prosperous without being dependent upon slave labor, and he is awed that "Every man appeared to understand his work, and went at it with a sober, yet cheerful earnestness, which betokened the deep interest which he felt in what he was doing, as well as a sense of his own dignity as a man."[29] At the conclusion of his narrative, he reflects on his own means of employment, which "was new, dirty, and hard work for me; but I went at it with a glad heart and a willing hand. I was now my own master. . . . It was the first work, the reward of which was to be entirely my own."[30] Here Douglass is showing how he has adopted an appreciation for the dignity of labor that he did not have when he was enslaved. This work ethic would later earn him wealth and influence, which he would describe in two subsequent autobiographies, *My Bondage and My Freedom* (1855) and *The Life and Times of Frederick Douglass* (1881, 1892), and which others, including Pauline Hopkins, would describe in their tributes to him.

In addition to autobiographical texts, a number of biographical diction- aries were produced in the nineteenth century that targeted an African American reading audience. Abigail Field Mott's *Biographical Sketches and Interesting Anecdotes of Persons of Color* (1837), which was intended to be used as a textbook in New York's "African Free Schools," presents sketches of Ignatius Sancho, Phillis Wheatley, Gustavus Vassa (Olauda Equino), and Toussaint L'Ouverture, along with sketches of local blacks, "to encourage virtue and morality in the different classes of society; and by bringing into view the effects which a system of slavery has on the human mind."[31] Mott's collection illustrates that early discourses about African American success focused more on Christian morality and less on material gain. Furthermore, antebellum literature defined African American success in terms of *physical freedom* as well as spiritual salvation. In the preface to this volume, Mott ex- plains, "The design of this selection is also to show the baneful effects of that degradation to which the children of Africa have, in an especial manner, been subjected by the Slave Trade; and to exhibit for encouragement and imitation, the salutary and cheering influence of the Christian religion."[32] Mott also reminds freed blacks that "by their good conduct they not only promote their own happiness, but that they advocate the cause of Universal Emancipation, by showing to the world their capability of enjoying the ben- efits of society, and providing comfortably for themselves."[33] It makes sense that before emancipation, freedom from bondage was routinely tied to the African American definition of success. Furthermore, a virtuous deport- ment not only ensured individual success but also contributed to the greater good of the black community as it was continuously judged according to the conduct of its members.

Once slavery was abolished, the black community turned its focus on achieving further progress, and success literature of the postbellum period reflected this shift in focus. For example, two of Booker T. Washington's post-Reconstruction autobiographies, *The Story of My Life and Work* (1900) and *Up From Slavery* (1901), revisit and revise a number of conventions of the antebellum slave narrative. I will devote more attention to Washington in the next chapter, but for now, it is worth noting that the story of his rise "up from slavery" through hard work, industry, and thrift to become the head of a successful educational institution and race leader is a self-conscious rendering of the gospel of success. Both white and black writers, including Washington, produced "conduct guides" for African American readers at the turn of the century. These lengthy books contained moral and ethical lessons on etiquette, health and hygiene, household management, and personal finance. They typically included elaborate engravings and were marketed door-to-door by traveling sales agents for the subscription publishing trade. *The College of Life, or Practical Self-Educator* is one example that contains sketches of prominent African American men but does not claim to be a simple biographical dictionary. Instead, according to its subtitle, it was offered as "A Manual of Self-Improvement for the Colored Race." This collaboration between Henry Davenport Northrop, Joseph R. Gay, and Irving Garland Penn was first published by the Chicago Publication and Lithograph Company in 1895, and it was reproduced by a number of other regional publishers, like W. A. Bruce of New York (1895), the Western Book Company of Denver (1896), and Philadelphia's National Publishing Company (1902). Northrop, a prolific white author, was already familiar to his contemporary readers, and Penn's name would have been readily recognized by anyone who knew of *The Afro-American Press and Its Editors*, which he published in 1891.

Just as Benjamin Franklin's writings illustrate the secular shift that took place in eighteenth- and nineteenth-century success literature, so does *College of Life* illustrate the increasing secularization of the success gospel at the turn of the twentieth century. In the introduction, the authors explain their desire to "advise, encourage and educate the many young people of the race and to inspire them with a desire to better their condition in life by Self-Improvement."[34] The profiles of notable black men and women included in the book provide "sketches of their achievements in life . . . as examples of what may be accomplished through education, patience, perseverance and integrity of character."[35] Conduct guides for African Americans presented black models for readers to emulate, but they typically did not radically politicize success. In this sense, *College of Life*'s objectives were very similar to Samuel Smiles's *Self-Help* (1859), an immensely popular book that was originally published in England and pirated numerous times abroad, including in the United States. According to Smiles, his book's "chief object unquestionably is to stimulate youths to apply themselves diligently to right pursuits . . . and to rely upon their own efforts in life, rather than depend upon the help or patronage of others."[36] Whereas the markings of success that Smiles identifies are "self-culture, self-discipline, self-control, [and] honest and up-

"Distinguished Colored Men," 1883 lithograph by George F. Crane. An example
of how accomplished African American men were celebrated in print. Courtesy of
Prints and Photographs Division, Library of Congress, LC-USZ62-7825.

right performance of individual duty, which is the glory of manly character," various selections in College of Life advocate the same universal values
of self-education, honesty, self-reliance, perseverance, industry and thrift,
patience, self-respect, and self-denial.[37] Furthermore, in the opening lines of
"The Guide to Success," a major section of College of Life, the authors discuss
success comparatively, claiming that blacks coveted the progress and standing that "others" have gained. "It has been truly said that great deeds and

examples inspire us to noble actions. We see what has been accomplished by others and we wish to be equally successful. We look at the enviable position they have gained and feel that we can become equally distinguished. We mark the respect they receive, the commendation given to them, the wide influence they are exerting, and our impulse is to make them a pattern for ourselves."[38] Not only did post-Reconstruction success literature for African Americans tend to depoliticize success, but it also tended to place the onus for overcoming the past disadvantages of slavery into the hands of the black community as they were given the charge of becoming upstanding American citizens. For example, the authors of *College of Life* seem particularly preoccupied with teaching their reading audience to be "the most useful members of society. We should be guided by right principles and prove ourselves worthy of the liberty granted us by emancipation."[39]

Pauline Hopkins was one turn-of-the-century black intellectual who was less concerned with proving that blacks were worthy of emancipation. While the authors of *College of Life* presented biographical sketches as evidence of the African American race's potential to succeed, Hopkins employed sketches of noteworthy blacks as evidence of the race's past and *ongoing* achievement. A close analysis of Hopkins's articles in the *Colored American Magazine* and *New Era Magazine* reveals that she realized the traditional gospel of success did not reflect the political, social, and economic conditions of the majority of African Americans, nor did it factor in the impact of discrimination or racism on a black person's ability to follow the common proscription for success. Her project took on visionary characteristics when she discussed African American success in a manner that was much more politicized than her contemporaries. Furthermore, the thematic content of her nonfiction is notable because of its sustained adaptation of the American success myth to the unique social circumstances of the black middle-class community.

"Famous Men of the Negro Race" is a series of twelve articles that recounts the accomplishments of historical and contemporary black men. While individual biographical pieces like Daniel Murray's "Cyrus Field Adams" and John Livinston Wright's "Charles W. Chesnutt" were dispersed throughout the volumes of the *Colored American Magazine*, "Famous Men" may well have been the first *series* of its kind to appear in a black monthly periodical with a national audience. Compared with the sketches in *College of Life*, Hopkins's "Famous Men" installments are more thorough; yet, what makes her treatment of these figures distinctive is the political commentary she weaves into them. Whereas the tone of *College of Life* and similar works implies that white culture and models of success are the most superior, Hopkins's writing is grounded on the premise that white models are flawed.

Consider, for example, the difference between Hopkins's depiction of Toussaint L'Ouverture and those of her contemporaries. In *College of Life*, the authors qualify their discussion of L'Ouverture, one example of "brilliant military genius," by reassuring their audience that blacks as a whole are not a violent people who seek "military glory."[40] L'Ouverture is characterized as a leader who assumed command of the Haitian revolution to achieve peace, not to conquer the French. The description of his noble character warrants quoting: "By the sheer force of his native ability and integrity he rose to the highest position among his people, and it is not too much to say that no nobler leader ever marshaled an army or struggled for independence. Not merely great military genius, not merely great ability as a statesman appeared in his marvelous career, but above all his exalted character shone resplendently, and he was too honest to be bribed, too courageous to surrender, and too devoted to the welfare [of] his race to count his life dear to him."[41] Here, this martyr's virtuous character is celebrated more than his military achievements. His instruction to his son to "forget that France murdered your father" is repeated twice in this very short sketch as if to emphasize his lack of bitterness or desire for vengeance against his French captors.[42] Hopkins begins her piece by signifying on previous depictions of L'Ouverture, like the one included in *College of Life*, by arguing in the head note that his "extraordinary fortunes . . . bespeak for him more than the passing interest of a dry biography."[43] She presents a more thorough treatment of her subject by including a geography lesson and history of slavery in Haiti in order to establish a context for the installment. Hopkins challenges the lowly position assigned to black people and their "supposed inferiority" by seeking "the ray of light in history that reveals the God in man; the divine attribute that must exist in the Negro as well as in other races, or he sinks to the level of the brute creation" (10). For Hopkins, L'Ouverture exemplifies how black people are just as intelligent, capable, and honorable as whites (if not more so), and that they have a history that accounts for these virtues. Hopkins does regret that L'Ouverture was profoundly loyal to France as she explains "the ruin of Toussaint was due in great measure to his loyalty to France and his filial feeling for Bonaparte."(16). Yet his dedication to a higher, more moral cause shows the breadth and depth of his discipline and self-control, for "It is no small evidence of Toussaint's greatness, then, that he enforced during such times such a principle as *no retaliation*." (17). Whereas Northrop, Gay, and Penn simply call L'Ouverture "the Napoleon Bonaparte of his race," Hopkins takes this comparison one step further and refers to him as "Napoleon's black shadow," which connotes his powerful leadership.[44] In essence, she crafts this portrait in a manner that motivates blacks and at the same time advocates in favor of the recognition she believed they deserved.

C. K. Doreski has analyzed the manner in which Hopkins used "Famous Men of the Negro Race" to reshape race history. Doreski observes that the *Colored American Magazine*, of which Hopkins was an instrumental contributor, "schooled its readers in arts and manners, hoping to provide that surface of success expected in the emerging middle class. But it also advanced a politically charged, cultural agenda in its challenge to the status quo and its commitment to the discovery and preservation of African American history."[45] While I do agree with Doreski's assessment of Hopkins as a historian and biographer, I want to emphasize how Hopkins's biographies did more than serve "a larger historical project" or were "a means of shaping race history"[46]; they were also conduits to promote her vision of African American success in the present and future. Furthermore, Hopkins was distinctive not only because of her political commentary, but also because of her *sustained* publications in the area of success, individual and community uplift, and race progress. Even though *College of Life* and similar works were reprinted in multiple editions, the authors typically wrote only one success guide. Hopkins, however, addressed the theme of success and progress repeatedly throughout her writing career. On the surface, Hopkins's definition of success appears the same as the traditional model in which an individual labors independently to achieve personal success. Hopkins consistently included the element of racial uplift, however, that not only made the success archetype more germane for African Americans, but also highlighted the role social environment played in one's ability to succeed in the United States. When not focused on individual success stories, white writers directed their attention to the progress of the nation to which the individual belonged. According to Samuel Smiles, "National progress is the sum of individual industry, energy, and uprightness, as national decay is of individual idleness, selfishness, and vice."[47] Hopkins bridged the gap between considerations of the individual and the nation by holding individuals accountable to the nation *and* to local communities. Hopkins's gospel of success called for African Americans to work cooperatively to ensure that the black individual and the black community achieve progress, and by modifying the success paradigm in this way, she implicitly responded to white oppression and also offered African Americans an alternative success model that embraced African American culture. In her nonfiction, she adopted and altered the traditional success formula and constructed a paradigm apropos of the African American experience by gauging the impact of race, racism, and the black community on the life of a successful black man. Rather than completely subscribe to the traditional definition of success, Hopkins deemphasized the materialism and competition characteristic of the secular model and placed more emphasis on making social contributions to one's local community. Further examination of Hopkins's biographical sketches reveals that Hopkins defined success not only in terms of the extent to which a man had been able to overcome hardship, increase his net worth, and acquire fame and social acceptance, but also by the degree to which he acted to help others, especially people of color. Furthermore, the level of social respectability Hopkins's successful man achieved revolved around how much he interacted with white people in a positive or influential way.

In the traditional model, a successful white man did not need to be socially accepted in black society. This attitude is reflected in the numerous writings that omit references to race or ethnicity, like Smiles's aforementioned *Self-Help*. In noting the absences of people of color from *Self-Help*, Peter Sinnema observes, "Smiles's attention is concentrated overwhelmingly on industrialists, artists, soldiers, and inventors from north-western Europe, particularly Great Britain, France, and Germany—industrialized, 'progressive' nations. . . . Smiles ignores altogether the heroic myths and legacies of aboriginal Africa, Asia, and the Indian subcontinent. These lands are represented simply as the terrain in which soldiers, colonists, and imperial administrators can energetically pursue glory, usually in the name of empire."[48] Only three "explicitly non-white men" are included in *Self-Help*: "Holkar of India, demonized as an enemy of the British Raj; Muley Moluc, the 'Moorish leader'; and Timur-i-Lan, the great Turkick general."[49] Thus, when Hopkins quotes Smiles in her exposé of the New York subway system and writes, "All nations have been made what they are by the thinking and working of many generations of men. Patient and persevering laborers in all ranks and conditions of life . . . all have contributed towards the grand result, one generation building upon another's labors, and carrying them forward to still higher stages," she revisits the issue of human progress but places it in a social context that Smiles fails to do, reminding readers at the end of the article that racial inequality continues to persist in spite of the city's technological achievements ("New York Subway," 605).

Hopkins's journalism, particularly the two series "Famous Men of the Negro Race" in the *Colored American Magazine* and "Men of Vision" in *New Era Magazine*, spoke to the black community's need for successful male role models and promoted her definitions of African American success and the black success archetype. "Famous Men of the Negro Race" consists of sketches of abolitionists, attorneys, politicians, educators, and other men who had a positive impact on the black community. Two articles in the "Men of Vision" series cover "the lives of those men of the race who have clearly demonstrated by their achievement that they are really 'Men of Vision'"

("Mark Rene Demortie," 35). Throughout both series and a number of other articles, Hopkins maintained her commitment to provide her audience with models of success. For example, in "Men of Vision: No. 2. Rev. Leonard Andrew Grimes," she argues that the life story she is offering to the reader "is a splendid example of successful individual effort working for the uplift of others are well as of self" (99). Individuals who were successful helped make the race successful in three ways. First, successful men served as role models for black youth. Throughout the "Famous Men" series, Hopkins comments on the potential her subject's life story has for motivating others. For example, in "Hon. Frederick Douglass," she writes, "He presents to us in his life an example of possibilities which may be within the reach of many young men of the rising generation" (132). In Lewis Hayden's biography, Hopkins argues that "The deeds of men of a past generation are the beacon lights along the shore for the youth of today" (476). Furthermore, of Robert Morris, she writes, "His life is a rich legacy to point the young Negro to the heights of manhood" (342). Second, these men helped uplift the race by using their power and influence to help those less fortunate than they were. For example, after recounting how Mark Rene Demortie used his influence to secure higher wages for black soldiers during the Civil War, Hopkins concludes, "So ends the record of an active life of love for humanity" (39). Third, the accomplishments of successful black men proved to whites they had already earned their place among the other United States citizens. In William Wells Brown's sketch, for example, Hopkins states, "In himself he was a refutation of the charge of the inferiority of the Negro" (232). Of Robert Brown Elliott she argues, "By his achievements we prove that it is possible for a Negro to rise to great political eminence as well as a white man. . . . Robert Elliott's life story is interwoven inseparably with the political history of the United States in the most critical period of its existence" (301). Hopkins linked the individual and the race's successes in response to the debate over whether or not blacks could "catch up" to other races on the hierarchal chain of civilization. In Lewis Hayden's sketch she argues, "The question then was: Has the Negro a right to resist his master? We settled that in the Civil War. The question now is: Has the Negro a right to citizenship?" (447). For Hopkins and other black intellectuals of this period, the black man's success had already answered this question and also indicated that the entire race earned and deserved its citizenship. In the following mission statement for the "Famous Men" series, Hopkins explains:

> We delight to honor the great men of our race because the lives of these noble Negroes are tongues of living flame speaking in the powerful silence of example, and sent to baptize the race with heaven's

holy fire into the noble heritage of perfected manhood. The contemplation of the life-work of these men is about all that we have to cheer and encourage us in our strivings after high ideals, and to appease our longings for the perfect day of our true emancipation—the black man's sweet but ever-vanishing vision of the Holy Grail. ("Robert Morris" 337)

Again, not only were these articles intended as examples of black achievement for white readers, they were also motivators for black readers.

At the turn of the century, African Americans realized whites often judged the entire black race by the actions of a few individuals. Meier explains, "If whites believed Negroes to be inferior, then Negroes must show themselves the equals of whites—by publicizing their past achievements, by successfully running the race of Social Darwinist competition with the whites, and by cultivating a vigorous racial pride to offset the Anglo-Saxon consciousness of kind."[50] Following in the tradition of Thomas Carlyle, Ralph Waldo Emerson, and Samuel Smiles, Hopkins wrote of the achievements of a select group of men, but she did this to remind her white and black readers of the role blacks have played in shaping American history and to provide models for her young black readers to emulate. Successful men were known to be the creators of history, the originators of a civilization. Thomas Carlyle believed that the actions of "great men" reflected on the greatness of a people. Because current leaders had failed society, Carlyle instructed people to worship past heroes by looking to their wisdom for guidance and direction. He also believed that the universal history of man's accomplishments was derived from the history of great men: "Captains of Industry are the true Fighters . . . Fighters against Chaos, Necessity and the Devils and Jotuns; and lead on Mankind in that great, and alone true, and universal warfare; the stars in their courses fighting for them, and all Heaven and all Earth saying audibly, Well done!"[51] Hopkins echoes these sentiments when she writes, "Races should be judged by the great men they produce, and by the average value of the masses. Races are tested by their courage, by the justice which underlies all their purposes, by their power and endurance—the determination to die for the right, if need be," but she also modifies his world view by writing about black heroes and representative men ("Toussaint L'Overture" 11–12). Because of the accomplishments of successful men like John Mercer Langston, Hopkins argues, the "history of the race is brighter, our position loftier for the example of his life and work" (177). Furthermore, "The heroic spirit in man, we therefore deduce, is the foundation of universal history, history itself being but an account of the deeds of men who have been the models and patterns for the great mass of humanity in past centuries even from the beginning of the world." ("Heroes and Heroines" 206)

Both Hopkins and traditional success writers used the self-made man's humble beginnings to gauge how far he had moved up in the world. According to the traditional model, a successful man typically originated from a modest background, often from rural surroundings, and from a harsh environment that consisted of poverty and an absentee father. Theodore Greene explains that, "When an American felt he must 'certainly know whether he was born man enough to win a prize in the struggle for life,' the only meaningful success was one achieved in spite of obstacles. Consequently, the childhood environment of the biographical hero was usually a picture of many hardships."[52] When Hopkins added a subtitle to Charles Winter Wood's biography, "or, From Bootblack to Professor," she signaled to her readers that the subject had risen from a modest background to a prestigious career. Wood was born in the South and at age nine migrated to Chicago. There he polished shoes and sold newspapers until he attracted the attention of a judge who helped him obtain a college education. Hopkins invokes her readers' sympathy by emphasizing the hardships Wood faced as a young boy in the city: "Is there a more touching sight, or one that appeals more strongly to the sympathetic soul, than that of a little child, claiming kindred with none, going about the business of bread-winning at an age when a loving mother trembles to have her darling exposed to the perils of the busy streets without the support of a strong guiding hand?" (345) She continues by arguing that because of his race, a black child on the street has a harder life than a white child, for "Such conditions are hard for a white child to overcome; many succumb and are overcome. How much harder are the same conditions when faced by one covered with the dark skin of the despised Negro!" (345). If two children are placed in the same circumstances, she posits, the black child will suffer more because of his race.

One of the most consequential hardships experienced by black people was slavery. By 1900, a significant portion of the black population were either formerly enslaved or one generation removed from slavery, and the men Hopkins selected for her series reflect this characteristic of the general black population. Seven of her sixteen subjects had been enslaved and another two men were the sons of former slaves. For Hopkins, one of the reasons why L'Ouverture was considered a success, despite his eventual capture by Napoleon's forces, is that he rose from slavery to lead a rebellion with slaves who did not possess military training or have advanced weapons. Writing about the achievements of great soldiers throughout history, she makes the following observation:

All these things were done by men of education capable of thinking and acting for themselves; with a long line of ancestry, perhaps,
which transmitted to its later offspring the power to command
armies and hold the reins of government. But think of the rise of
the Haytian [sic] slaves under a slave! armed with nothing but their
implements of toil and their own brave hearts, who out of their
mountains and running streams forged the arms that drove back the
conqueror of the world; and clasping Freedom to her breast, Hayti
[sic] crowned herself with the cap of liberty. (24)

Other ex-slaves who rose from bondage to achieve great accomplishments
include Frederick Douglass, who survived "bad treatment and frequent
whippings" as a child (121), and William Wells Brown, who "accomplished
an almost impossible task in surmounting the training received in slavery"
(232). John Mercer Langston, a successful lawyer and founder of Howard
University's law school, was not only an ex-slave but had also been orphaned
when he was five years old. Hopkins may appear to minimize the trauma
of slavery when she uses phrases like "bad treatment" and "frequent whippings" to describe the slaves' experiences, but in actuality, she was recasting
these well-known biographies into the form of a rags-to-riches tale to give
these hardships a new significance. In the past, details about the brutality
of slavery would have been used to argue for its abolition. Here, Hopkins
used these biographies as encouragement to show how men who suffered
through the unique hardships of slavery could overcome them through hard
work and perseverance. "Well, the Negro is used to hard conditions," she
contends, "he will come out all right if he has patience and endurance—and
doesn't starve while waiting for Americans to arouse themselves to a full
perception of the wrongs inflicted on the most inoffensive class of citizens
in the Republic" ("Charles Winter Wood" 345). Even black men who were
born free experience hardship stemming from American racism and segregation. Hopkins makes a point of reminding her readers of this when she
argues that "The modern colored citizen is afflicted by segregation, even as
the old-timers were by slavery—ostracism and its attendant evils, the humili-
ating knowledge that, in general, the public on the highway, in assemblies
and employment, shrink from us as from contaminating lepers" ("Leonard
Andrew Grimes" 99). Hence, the abolitionist Leonard Grimes was also born
of free parents, but he was still "subjected to all the disabilities that his race
had to endure at the South" (99). He was orphaned at an early age, like John
Mercer Langston, and he struggled through an unhappy childhood until he
moved to Washington, D.C. Although Mark Demortie, famous abolitionist

and politician, was a free-born black man, "that was a signal disadvantage," argues Hopkins; "free-born colored men of his time were hampered by every difficulty attending life" (35). Furthermore, Robert Morris's life is an example of " . . . accomplishment from the barest possibilities" (337).

After overcoming obstacles and hardship, another indication of an individual's attainment of success was whether or not he became famous. According to Greene, fame and notoriety were important elements of the late nineteenth-century success model: "Personal fame achieved by powerful individuals who 'made an impress' on their environment emerges as the dominant goal for these years."[53] Furthermore, Huber explains that success meant achieving recognition for one's accomplishments: "Recognition was the nerve of success—recognition measurable in money or applause."[54] Although Hopkins deemphasized the importance of wealth, fame was a key factor in her version of success. Hopkins wrote about black men whose notoriety may not have been recognized in the white press but who were famous in the black community. Often their fame was achieved by working to uplift the race in some manner. For example, she argues that the Haitian slave revolt led by L'Ouverture deserves more recognition and "ought to have a world-wide fame. It stands without a parallel in history—the successful uprising of slaves against their masters, and the final establishment of their independence" (14). Frederick Douglass was a successful individual whose personal fame had a positive impact on the black community, and "An honored name is his bequest to the Negro of the United States" (132). William Wells Brown was "widely known both at home and abroad" (232). Hopkins notes that as an abolitionist and author, "Doctor Brown was the recipient of many congratulations on his work as an author, and the British press vied with their American brothers in doing honor to this new star in the world of letters" (233). Robert Brown Elliott was famous for speeches that he made while serving terms in Congress, particularly on the civil rights bill. Furthermore, in terms of John Mercer Langston's fame, Hopkins claims that

> [t]here is no part of the United States where the name of the late John M. Langston is unknown, where his brilliant career is not pointed to with pride by the Afro-American, for he loved his friends, his country, and his race.
>
> His books, his speeches, his professional career as a lawyer and as an educator, his last and most conspicuous efforts as a statesman, endear him to the lowliest in the walks of life as well as to the highest in culture and social prominence. The history of the race is brighter, our position loftier for the example of his life and work. (177)

Langston was famous for many black firsts that included being the first black theological student in the United States, the first black lawyer in Ohio, and the first black man elected to an office by popular vote, the achievement of which "gave him name and fame all over the country, and he was immediately invited by the American Anti-Slavery Society to address a meeting at the Metropolitan Theatre, New York City" (180).

In addition to fame, another indication that a black man had achieved success was the extent to which he was socially accepted and could use his acquired power to influence others. Although all blacks suffered from segregation and Jim Crow laws, all of Hopkins's self-made men were socially accepted in some way that transcended these barriers. For Hopkins, self-made men like Robert Elliott and Edwin Garrison Walker were noteworthy because they used their influence with whites to improve sociopolitical conditions for the African American community. Toussaint L'Ouverture stood out for a number of reasons: "Under his paternal administration, law, morals, religion, education and industry were in full force, while commerce and agriculture flourished. *No retaliation* was the command of this ex-slave to his generals; and no one was so severely dealt with as those who infringed upon this order" (17). Frederick Douglass's skill as a lecturer gave him power: "White men and black men had spoken on slavery but never like Frederick Douglas. . . . He made his audiences weep, laugh, swear. He opened the hearts of thousands to mercy and pity for the slave by his eloquence and paths. Many kept away from his lectures lest they be converted against their will" (124). Furthermore, Douglass was also successful because he was respected by both blacks and whites: "As a freeman and a citizen the respect of mankind has been heaped upon his head, and trusts of great honor have been laid in his lap by a great nation" (130). Thus, Douglass served many political appointments, for example, as a diplomat to Haiti. In terms of Charles Lenox Remond's influence, Hopkins claims that it is "with us today, ruling us by example from beyond the grave" (38). In addition, Langston's influence extends beyond the American people: "Mr. Langston, as the chief representative of the United States in Hayti [sic], is so imbued with the spirit of American institutions, that a personal influence goes out from him that is producing a salutary effect on the Haytian [sic] people and government to the endless credit of the American nation and people" (82). Other men who received political appointments include Blanche K. Bruce, who was appointed to the office of Register of the Treasury by President Garfield (258), and John Mercer Langston, who was appointed by President Hayes to the Office of Minister-Resident and as Consul-General to Haiti. Mark Demortie was appointed "deputy collector of internal revenue" (38). In short, political appointments combated stereotypes of blacks being corrupt or too incompetent to serve in the government. For William Wells Brown, his success and degree of social acceptance was indicated by the invitations he received from the white nobility while on tour in Great Britain: "His reception was most flattering; his address created a profound sensation. At its conclusion the speaker was warmly greeted by Victor Hugo, president of the Congress, and many other distinguished men" (233). Charles Remond was also well-received in England and was even befriended by Lady Byron. Interestingly, Edwin Garrison Walker was respected by other minorities that traditionally held tense relations with blacks: "Lawyer Walker honored the Irish voter, and was a member of a secret order of Irishmen, himself the only black man in it" (364). Of Lewis Hayden, Hopkins notes that "at his death [he] held the respect of all persons—white and black—from the governor down to the lowliest citizen of the grand old commonwealth of Massachusetts" (473). Finally, Hopkins makes a brief but significant comment about how Sgt. William Carney was "highly respected by all citizens" (88).

By far the most telling confirmation of a black man achieving success arrived when he had a successful business with both black and white clients. As Butler notes in his economic detour theory, having customers outside one's race was an indication of surmounting the hurdle of gaining access to the open market economy.[55] Black business owners internalized interracial support to mean that they were providing services valued by white patrons. Hopkins observes that attorney John Mercer Langston successfully defended white clients: "Within less than one year after his admission to the Bar, his practice had become lucrative; his clients were all white. They sought him and his services as if they had full confidence in this ability" (179). Langston also taught white students at Howard Law School because of the growing reputation of his school: "As the name and character of the law department of the university became known, and the results of its training were made manifest, an increasing number of white students joined it, and pursued, with their colored associates, its regular course of study, many of them graduating with honor" (182). So, in an era of segregated and usually unequal educational systems, Langston built a school of such merit that white students were eager to attend. Furthermore, Robert Morris also had white clients: "Boston's Negro lawyer after this was continually in the public eye, and soon had as many criminal cases upon his docket as any other attorney in the county. He was, in fact, the favorite criminal lawyer of Suffolk bar. His clients were from the humble walks of life, white and colored, by far the greater number being white, and Irishmen" (340). Hopkins even includes testimony from a white judge that addresses Morris's social acceptance: "It is often said that Mr. Morris deserves credit for what he did for his race. I thank him for what he did for ours. While it is sad to be the victim of low prejudice, it is worse to be its slave, and Robert Morris did a man's work toward emancipating the white men of this community from that yoke" (340). Such remarks from a white, prominent man about a black man rarely appeared in the mainstream press.

As noted above, the extent to which wealth is used to define one's success varies, but some increase in financial status is part of the traditional model. For Hopkins, wealth was not key to African American success, the way social acceptance and influence were. Interestingly, Hopkins rarely comments on her subjects' financial status, and when she does, it is often in passing, for the purpose of showing how the individual sacrifices personal gain for the benefit of the black community, or it is tied to some other element of success like social acceptance. For example, Frederick Douglass's opulent Washington, D.C., home was formerly owned by a white man: "His villa was one of the finest and most desirable in the Republic, whose original proprietor stipulated in the deed of transfer that the property should never be owned by a descendant of the African race" (131). Yet, the deed was transferred to Douglass, one assumes, because of his fame and social stature. Hopkins informs her audience that Lewis Hayden used his wealth to help John Brown: "He might have been wealthy, for he possessed the faculty of making money, but he scattered it broadcast to help those poorer than himself" (476). Hopkins makes passing reference to Booker T. Washington's "humble birth and rise to eminence and wealth" (441), while Demortie "raised himself to power and wealth by force of character alone" (35). Grimes passed up opportunities to make a "large salary" when he turned down a job offer to be an overseer. Instead, he set up a business as a hack man, where "He prospered and was soon well known in that line of business" and earned a moderate income through hard work (100). According to Hopkins, "His carriages were in demand by the wealthiest people of the Capital and at the same time he was assisting fugitives to the North or to Canada" (100). Perhaps her most interesting and clear position on wealth is found in her article on William Pickens in which she frowns upon the lavish gifts that she calls "temptations" bestowed upon this successful Yale student by white patrons. First, President Roosevelt's sister offers Pickens financial assistance. Second, a millionaire's daughter is so moved by one of his speeches that she sticks a diamond pin in his coat. And finally, a committee from Harvard University and the city of Boston meets Pickens at the train station in a barouche. Hopkins quips, "This is a pretty strong dose of adulation" (518). Hopkins's criticism of this attention suggests Pickens had not earned these things through hard work or labor, as her model dictates.

Instead of being judged by the amount of money they make, Hopkins's successful men on the whole were esteemed for their social contributions, especially for their efforts to uplift the race. Six of the sixteen men were abolitionists, or at least helped fugitive slaves escape their captors. L'Ouverture, Douglass, Wells Brown, Hayden, Remond, and Grimes all helped the slave population in varying degrees—from leading a slave rebellion to saving fugitive slaves from mob violence. Robert Brown Elliott was noted for helping establish the first public school system in South Carolina. Lewis Hayden's social contributions extended beyond providing a safe haven for the fugitive slaves William and Ellen Crafts; according to Hopkins, "Lewis Hayden's greatness came from his love of his race and the sacrifices he made of money, of time and of physical comfort for the redemption of a people from chattel bondage" (474). Robert Morris personally fought discrimination and northern segregation in Boston public schools, the railroad system, theaters, churches "and other public places" (341). He lobbied for black officers and equal pay for black troops during the Civil War. Morris risked his life to save a fugitive slave from imprisonment by rescuing him from the courtroom and helping him on his way to Canada. Mark Demortie, like Robert Morris, also worked to desegregate Boston's public school system. His long list of racial uplift activities includes helping to get the ethnic designation "colored" removed from voting lists, working to get equal pay for black Civil War troops, establishing more black schools in Virginia, and lobbying to get antilynching legislation introduced to Congress. Hopkins emphasized these individuals' community service years before white success writers are willing to give more credence to the self-made man's social contributions to society. Although there were some murmurs in the late 1890s about the level of individualism being emphasized in the success formula, according to Greene, "All the major means to success in this decade remained individualistic ones. . . . The accumulating emphasis on his quest for Personal Fame, on the forceful character he displayed, on his domination of others, on the childhood obstacles he overcame, and on the masterful tactics he employed all centered attention on the individual himself."[56] Furthermore, "To intimate that development was fostered by cooperation rather than competition, to suggest that success was social rather than individual, this was going far beyond the admission that opportunities had to be provided by the environment."[57] Yet, this admission is exactly what Hopkins advocated in these biographical articles and in her attempt to define success by the degree to which black men helped others to achieve. Doreski makes a similar observation: "Hopkins sought to enlighten and inspirit readers into a kindred abolitionist fervor by using social and cultural exemplars to nullify competing racist ideologies. Unlike her transcendentalist models, she sought not to privilege the individual but to celebrate an evolving sense of historical integrity and community."[58]

Corresponding with her definition of success, the virtues of Hopkins's self-made man share some characteristics with the traditional archetype, but Hopkins added specific traits to give racial significance to these characteristics and to highlight the special political and social circumstances blacks face in the United States. Like the traditional success model, Hopkins's self-made men possessed natural intelligence, high ethical and moral standards, honor, determination, and self-reliance. Unlike the white model, Hopkins's model also had a strong commitment to racial uplift.

First, the black self-made man was naturally intelligent and was precocious as a child. Whether he received a formal education or was self-taught, he understood the value of education. Recounting a man's birth, parentage, and educational background is the pattern of biographical writing, but Hopkins emphasizes that these black men were highly intelligent. Thus, John Mercer Langston had private tutors from Oberlin College, attended theological school, and was eventually the first black lawyer in Ohio. He possessed a "wonderfully fertile mind" and "genius accompanied by skill, good sense, [and] a well-balanced mind" (180). Senator Blanche K. Bruce was born a slave and "received the rudiments of an education from the tutor of his master's son"; but the "thirst for knowledge would not be appeased . . . and his longings soon turned his footsteps toward Oberlin College, the intellectual nurse of so many black men of eminence and renown" (258). Lewis Hayden "was endowed with a great mind although lacking the training of cultivation. But what of that? We have lived to prove the truth of the aphorism: Great minds are not made in schools" (473). Charles Winter Wood progressed from menial labor to a high position in academia: "All the capital of the street child lies in his precocious brain, and his keen analysis of human nature which enables him to charm the coin from the pockets of the passing throng by any means most favorable" (345). After migrating from Nashville to Chicago, Wood's natural street smarts helped him survive. At the age of twelve he recited a scene from *Hamlet* for one of his customers. Eventually this customer provided Wood with a formal education, and for a time "the young genius" (346) was the only black student at Beloit College. Wood also entered postgraduate studies at Chicago Theological Seminary and Columbia University. These examples are significant because blacks have been stereotyped as intellectually inferior, and intellectual precocity in blacks was considered odd. In Wood's case, white lawyers and judges gathered to hear him recite Shakespeare and pay him for entertaining them. Yet, Wood made the best use of his talent and secured a formal education that helped him become a successful English professor at Tuskegee University.

Hopkins's self-made man had high ethical and moral standards, deep conviction, and was even willing to die for his cause. These traits combated racist stereotypes and assumptions that blacks lacked morals. As Hopkins says when writing about Toussaint L'Ouverture: "Races should be judged by the great men they produce, and by the average value of the masses. Races are tested by their courage, by the justice which underlies all their purposes, by their power and endurance—the determination to die for the right, if need be" (11–12). If blacks were judged by L'Ouverture's courage and the "purity of his purpose," they would be ranked higher in "the annals of history" (12). Hopkins says that William Wells Brown was "a man of deep conviction and unquenchable resolves, he could not remain idle" (232). Sergeant Carney was an officer in the Civil War and a member of the Fifty-fourth Regiment of Massachusetts Volunteer Infantry. During the battle at Fort Wagner in 1863, his regiment's color-sergeant was wounded. Carney managed to take possession of the flag before it fell to the ground. He was wounded carrying the flag, "But, on orders being given to retire, the color-bearer, though almost disabled, still held the emblem of liberty in the air. . . . Surely, the honor of Massachusetts was safe in such hands!" (87).

Hopkins's self-made man was determined and self-reliant. Robert Morris, for example, was determined "to be a man and a gentleman, and succeed in the practice of law" or die (339). While introducing Charles Lenox Remond's life story, Hopkins writes, "Ordinarily a biography is expected to begin with some genealogical narrative, intended to show that the person presented to the reader was descended from ancestors of renown. . . . But these men of the Negro race whom we delight to honor, had no ancestors. 'Self-made,' they traced their lineage from the common ancestor, Adam" (34–35). Here Hopkins turns a perceived weakness in a lack of documented familial history into a strength. And, in arguing that these men share Adam as their common ancestor, she gives them a lineage more privileged than any member of the famous Rockefeller family. Of John Mercer Langston, Hopkins writes, "Mr. Langston accomplished his own success in life. His determination was supreme. His motto, 'SELF-RELIANCE THE SECRET OF SUCCESS.' His perseverance, self-trust, were as great as the decision of his will. . . . In these elements of firmness and unswerving resolution lie the essential principles of success, in every arduous undertaking for all men of all races" (184). Racial uplift through personal social contributions is key to African American success. Hopkins's self-made men were active in the black community, charitable, and had a propensity for performing unselfish acts to benefit the race. According to Cawelti, during the late nineteenth century many Americans believed that the personal "pursuit of economic advancement is not only to the individual's advantage, but the best way to help others" because economic expansion created more income opportunities for the general public.[59] For Hopkins, blacks directly helping each other was more advantageous for the black community than waiting for whites to accept what she perceived to be their responsibility to provide assistance to blacks. Though the traditional model includes charity work, most successful whites were politically conservative, giving money only to certain causes, and they did not express the same level of personal responsibility to their communities as blacks. Furthermore, during the late nineteenth century most people thought poverty was the result of sloth. People did not intervene on behalf of the poor unless they earned it: "In fact, many people believed, to qualify for financial assistance, a beneficiary had to earn respect and thus indicate loyalty, courage, and parity of spirit."[60] Here is one particular area where Hopkins redefined the archetype, making the participation in racial uplift a key characteristic of the self-made man. Robert Morris personally fought discrimination and segregation in Massachusetts by allowing himself to be thrown out of public places and then suing in court. Hopkins adds that "The most heroic proof of his devotion to his race, was given during the trying time of the operation of the fugitive slave law" when Morris risked his own life to rescue African Americans who were being remanded back to slavery (341).

Realistically, no one individual possessed all of these traits; for example, some were formally educated and others were not. So, Hopkins used the entire series to build a composite of the self-made man. This increased the likelihood that a larger reading audience could identify with at least one of the multiple models of success. One should not dismiss Hopkins's courage in choosing black male figures to make the success paradigm applicable to blacks. At a time when Napoleon was a standard subject of success writing, she chose to chronicle the achievements of his adversary, L'Ouverture, instead. Hopkins's choice of hero here is telling, because the years 1894 to 1903 were "a Napoleon decade" and Napoleon symbolized "the successful individual."[61] While Napoleon's image was "the single most common stereotype in [white] magazine biographies of this decade," Hopkins Signified on this image by invoking the image of Toussaint.[62] Napoleon was popular because "It was also his embodiment of supreme individual force and his self-made rise from obscurity which fitted him for the role."[63] L'Ouverture also rose from obscurity, not to conquer but to free his country.

"Americans are fiercely proud of the opportunities which they believe their uniquely open society offers the average man," writes John Cawelti. "Every American boy has the chance to become President of the United States, or at least a wealthy businessman."[64] As we shall see in the following chapters, Hopkins expanded her project by using her fictional works to criticize these traditional beliefs by showing that in reality, not every American boy at the turn of the century had the chance to become president or a wealthy businessman. One American in particular, Booker T. Washington, was the target of Hopkins's direct and indirect criticism for his failure to acknowledge the limitations that were being placed on African Americans who were trying to fulfill their own American Dreams.

CHAPTER 2

Furnace Blasts for the Tuskegee Wizard and the Talented Tenth: Hopkins and Her Contemporary Self-Made Men

Pauline Hopkins was the most prolific black woman writer of her time. Her work with the *Colored American Magazine* played no small part in earning her this distinction, for she published three serialized novels and several short stories and editorial pieces in the magazine. She abruptly stopped editing and contributing to the magazine in 1904, however. Some literary historians have assumed she left because Booker T. Washington purchased the journal and replaced her with one of his allies, and they dismiss the end of her tenure there as merely a casualty of the Tuskegee Machine. Hopkins's contemporary, W. E. B. Du Bois, theorized, with little elaboration, that Hopkins "was not conciliatory enough" toward white readers.[1] In his 1947 version of the publication's history, William Stanley Braithwaite, who worked directly with Hopkins as one of the *Colored American Magazine*'s literary critics, chose not to comment on how readers responded to Hopkins's political ideas. Instead, he characterized Hopkins as a "temperamental editor" whose desire for "an independence of action in making selections, and a dignity in soliciting manuscripts of the best" caused "friction" in the magazine's work environment.[2] Considering his first-hand experiences with the magazine, Braithwaite's account is surprisingly devoid of details pertaining to the challenges Hopkins faced as she maneuvered the periodical publication process. As a result, scholars continue to speculate why she left and under what circumstances. For example, Jill Bergman has concluded that despite current trends that characterize Hopkins's cultural politics as radical, she was probably dismissed from her position because of gender bias and changes in the journal's management that shifted the publication's focus from a female to a male-centered audience.[3]

In the previous chapter, I discussed how Hopkins's success literature was more politicized than that of her contemporaries. Historicizing the lives of notable black figures enabled her to celebrate the past, present, and future achievements of African Americans and unapologetically demonstrate her race pride. In this chapter, I will show how Hopkins's defiant nature (which has either been misread or overlooked) and her radical ideology about the role of literature in the early twentieth-century racial uplift movement constitute a subversive subtext in the articles she wrote and the editorial decisions she made for the *Colored American Magazine*. Although current trends in Hopkins scholarship continue to focus on her magazine novels, especially *Of One Blood*, more attention is being directed at Hopkins's role as a magazine editor and at how she used her nonfiction writing to explore and educate her readership about a variety of issues, like the heroics of historical black figures and black women's participation in the club movement. More important, not only did Hopkins use her editorial position at the *Colored American Magazine* to advocate a particular success formula for African Americans that differed from the traditional formula, but she did this while protesting against Booker T. Washington's brand of racial uplift and his adaptation of the gospel of success.

Archival evidence in the Pauline Hopkins Collection at Fisk University's Franklin Library suggests that in addition to both Hopkins's race and gender politics, her insistence on producing a literary journal instead of a business or current events magazine put her at odds with Washington and his supporters. An examination of correspondence between Hopkins and John C. Freund, editor of a New York music trade magazine and a Washington supporter, reveals that Hopkins was in fact removed from her editorial position because of her radical anti-accommodationist views about the value of literature and higher education in the racial uplift movement. Hanna Wallinger has offered a different reading of the Hopkins correspondence that, I believe, focuses on her victimization and, as a result, misses Hopkins's deliberate and ultimately effective challenge of Washington's authority.[4] Taking Hopkins's articles, including but not limited to her "Famous Men of the Negro Race" series, into consideration helps the way in which she subverted Washington's sociopolitical agenda become more evident. In short, Hopkins's editorial policy not only opposed Washington but also put him on the defensive and precipitated her departure from the magazine. While Hopkins lost the battle for editorial control of the *Colored American Magazine*, she emerged as a force that Washington had to reckon with.

Hopkins's particular adoption and adaptation of the success archetype distinguished her from many pre–Harlem Renaissance intellectuals, especially Booker T. Washington, because it criticized United States policy regarding the "Negro Problem" in a way that promoted agitation for civil rights rather than the assimilation of Western cultural standards that subscribed to notions of black inferiority. Throughout her work, Hopkins continually called her readers' attention to social and political injustice in the North and South by detailing southern rape and lynching scenes and by explaining northern job discrimination practices. In addition, Hopkins critiqued the success archetype by using her writing to take to task the most powerful black leader at the turn of the century, and criticize his efforts to apply the traditional self-help model to his own life. Booker T. Washington was considered by many to be a black version of the self-made man. Phillipa Kafka's *The Great White Way* discusses "Booker T. Washington's lifelong attempt to expand the concept of American male success mythology in the workplace to include Black men."[5] I would add that Hopkins used her position at the magazine to conduct a controversial project of crafting in her nonfiction journalism to expose the limits of Washington's self-help program and his policies.

Black leaders and intellectuals differed in their opinions about the best way to obtain success for the African American population. Although most black leaders agreed with the theories of self-help, race pride, and uplift, they often disagreed about the best way to put these theories into practice. Booker T. Washington believed that blacks should remain in the South, where they would be successful in small business and artisan trades. By developing their skills in the trades, blacks would reclaim the monopoly of skilled labor that they had during slavery. "The central theme in Washington's philosophy," Meier explains, "was that through thrift, industry, and Christian character Negroes would eventually attain their constitutional rights." Washington also urged southern whites to help uplift blacks "out of economic self-interest," arguing that prosperous blacks would purchase property from whites and partner with them to develop the southern economy.[6] He criticized blacks who complained about their condition or sought an impractical liberal arts education in lieu of a practical industrial education that emphasized business development along with farming and trade professions. He did not encourage the black masses to seek the franchise, for he did not want to antagonize southern whites against black suffrage. Hopkins's program was different from Booker T. Washington's in a number of ways. Hopkins did not encourage blacks to remain in the South, and she constantly criticized southern social and political practices in her work. She argued that whites should be held accountable for their past involvement in slavery and their current participation in the continued oppression of African Americans. Hopkins believed the African American community needed to demand its civil rights, and especially its voting rights. Most important, she valued the study of literature and believed it served a purpose in encouraging the race to strive toward success. By publicly calling attention to previous and current wrongs incurred by African Americans, Hopkins was labeled an "agitator."

Hopkins's earliest critique of Booker T. Washington can be found in *Contending Forces*. She secured the copyright for the novel in 1899, which suggests she began writing it in 1898 or 1899. By the fall of 1900, when *Contending Forces* appeared in print, five years had passed since Washington delivered his Atlanta Exposition Address that catapulted him to the head of the country's black leadership. Also, by 1900, some people were second-guessing Washington's ideologies, and definitive camps of Washington's supporters (the "Bookerites") and detractors (the "anti-Bookerites") were forming. As a Boston resident, Hopkins worked in "the center of the most vehement agitation" for civil rights, and she wove this political climate into her novel.[7] Hopkins first depicts the Bookerite and anti-Bookerite positions during conversations between Dora Smith and Sappho Clark, the novel's two primary female characters, and does so again later in her portrayal of Dr. Arthur Lewis, president of a southern industrial school, and William Smith, an intellectual and Harvard graduate, nearly a decade before the "Washington–Du Bois debate" would escalate to its most tense moments. I believe a less obvious but equally important portrayal of Washington can be read in the characterization of John Langley, a duplicitous politician and Will's foil. Together, Arthur Lewis and John Langley form two faces of Booker T. Washington: the public face of Tuskegee's principal and the private face behind the Tuskegee Machine. A few other scholars, including John Gruesser, Julie Cary Nerad, and Erica Griffin, have given passing reference to Hopkins's treatment of the debate in *Contending Forces*.[8] Still, Hopkins's treatment of these two black leaders in her fiction warrants further discussion because it illustrates her foresight and intimate knowledge of key black intellectuals and political leaders.

Hopkins uses Dr. Arthur Lewis's character to portray Washington's public persona. Both men are in charge of southern industrial schools; while Washington was the principal of Tuskegee Normal and Industrial Institute in Alabama, Dr. Lewis is the head of the African School of Industrial and Agricultural Development in Louisiana.[9] Like Tuskegee, the campus of Lewis's school is self-sufficient and a showpiece of African American industry: "the numerous dormitories, museums, the chapel, and buildings which held lecture-rooms and class-rooms, were all built by the pupils of the school. The students made the brick which entered into the composition of the various buildings; the carpenter shop, carriage and blacksmith shops afforded fine facilities for imparting practical knowledge of these useful industries" (387–88). The school is also equipped with gardens and livestock "from all

Booker T. Washington, ca. 1895. Courtesy of Prints and Photographs Division, Library of Congress, LC-J694-255.

of which came some revenue to help defray the expenses of this human hive of industry" (388). According to Dora, Dr. Lewis's eventual wife, his position is "that industrial education and the exclusion of politics will cure all our race troubles" (124). Like Washington, Dr. Lewis opposes black enfranchisement and believes that it "would be better for us; the great loss of life would cease, and we should be at peace with the whites" if blacks did not exercise their right to vote (125). Dr. Lewis focuses on the economic advancement of blacks, believing that money and material gain will help them procure fairer treatment in the South. Dora tells Sappho, "but money makes the mare go. . . . I say to you, as Arthur says to me when I tell him what I think of his system. . . . When we can say that lots of our men are as rich as Jews, there'll be no question about the franchise" (126–27). Dora, a very likable character, defends Dr. Lewis's/Washington's position by explaining, "But you see his is living South [sic]; his work is there, and he must keep in with the whites of the section where his work lies, or all he has accomplished will go for naught, and perhaps his life might be forfeited, too" (126). Later in the novel Hopkins further proposes that Lewis is a product of his environment. At the Canterbury Club dinner, the narrator comments:

> He had accomplished great things; had made himself the center of this terrible human tragedy in the heart of the Black Belt, where the college was situated; but the deadly antagonism of the South made even his iron-hearted stoicism bow to its tyrannical decrees, insomuch that he had been forced to compromise, and the educational advantages allowed the pupils had been curtailed to suit the views of those who placed a low estimate on the ability of the Negro, in spite of the many bright examples of superior intellectual endowments which exist among them. (288)

The authorial voice suggests that Washington's tactics may be acceptable in the South, but they are not appropriate for northern blacks, where

> The colored people north of Mason and Dixon's line are conspicuous for their advancement along all the lines which are distinctive features in the formation of the polished exterior of the good citizen of such a republic as ours. Among the best circles of this community are found the highest types of intellectual, moral, religious and social improvement. What becomes of such a class as this when hampered by rules and laws made to fit the needs of the Black Belt? laws [sic] of life and living which cannot be forced, and ought not to be forced, upon the large class of colored citizens who embody within themselves the highest development of American citizenship? (289)

Thus, in this novel, Hopkins poses questions about the appropriateness of Washington's policy for northern blacks.

Though Hopkins does not depict the public Washington in a manner that would attack him personally, she is clearly opposed to Washington's underhanded political maneuverings, and here is where John Langley's embodiment of this other side of Washington is significant. Interestingly, Hazel Carby does not make the connection between Washington and Langley, but she does notice that "Hopkins molded Langley as an archetype, an embodiment of the cultural myth of the rise of the poor child to success and power. She re-created in this individual character what she understood to be a representative figure of the 'Gilded Age,' manipulating and monopolizing unbridled power."[10] The similarities between Washington and Langley are striking. Washington came from a life of slavery and then poverty as a child laborer in the salt furnaces and coal mines of West Virginia. Like Washington, John travels far from home and arrives in his new destination with no money, "a half-starved beggar in the city streets, a deserted child claiming kindred with none, allowed a shelter in a poor Negro cabin for charity's sake, begging his bread from the generous passer-by" (335). Also like Washington, Langley's education is important to him and he leaves home as a child seeking formal instruction, and he works to cover his educational expenses. Langley is most like Washington when it comes to his political activities in that he discourages blacks from participating in politics while he himself makes deals and compromises with white politicians. Midway through the novel, a southern black man is brutally lynched for allegedly raping a white woman. During a conversation with Hon. Herbert Clapp, a white politician and southern sympathizer, Langley's defense of the black community is so out of character for him that even Clapp notices. Clapp asks Langley what he (and the black community) wants, and Langley replies that blacks deserve to be more than bootblacks, which is a hypocritical statement because he will not hire black employees. By the end of the meeting, Langley sells out his own race by discouraging the black community from agitating over the recent lynching in exchange for a political office as city solicitor. Many scholars acknowledge the fact that Washington had two personas: a public one and a private one. Meier has called Washington a "powerful politician in his own right" and has given examples of his *clandestine* political activities.[11] For example, he discouraged blacks from entering politics, but he also advised President Roosevelt on several political appointments, both white and black.[12] He fought in favor of blacks by lobbying against the 1899 Georgia disfranchisement bill and railroad segregation while retaining high esteem of white philanthropists who donated money to black schools.[13] But there was an even darker side to Washington. As he became increasingly sensitive to criticism from the black community, "He used every means at his disposal to combat his critics—his influence with the press, placing spies in the opposition movements, depriving their members of church and political positions."[14] It is not clear how much of Washington's clandestine tactics Hopkins was aware of when she wrote *Contending Forces*, but she did question the state of black leadership at a moment when Washington was considered at the height of political power and influence. In *Contending Forces*, she writes, "In the present emergency which confronts us as a race, no leader has yet pressed forward to take command, as in those glorious old days" of the abolitionist movement (277). This authorial comment is strategically placed in a chapter that centers around Langley's political maneuverings. Ultimately, Langley does not fit Hopkins's model of success because he does not help uplift his community. He obtains an education, but "He had accomplished the acquisition of knowledge at the expense of the non-development of every moral faculty" (335). Furthermore, "John had given no thought to the needs of his soul in his pursuit of wealth and position" (336). He does not help uplift his community even though he is an executive officer of the American Colored League. Langley is in a position to help other blacks, but he hires a white office boy and stenographer instead of giving blacks the opportunity to work for him. Langley is not a true race man; rather, he is the antithesis of the successful lawyers that Hopkins features in her "Famous Men" series. Even though white clients are an indication of success, for Hopkins, having white employees at the expense of blacks is not a sign of progress.

While the novel's antagonist is imbued with Booker T. Washington's less than admirable qualities, *Contending Forces* hero, Will Smith, is given traits that we would readily identify with Washington's eventual adversary, W. E. B. Du Bois. For instance, the men share very similar educational backgrounds. In addition to graduating from Fisk University in 1888, Du Bois earned degrees from Harvard University in 1890 and 1895 and studied at the University of Berlin. Will, likewise, is depicted as "a brilliant philosophical student" who studies at Harvard and then the University of Heidelberg (166). Will and Du Bois also share comparable views on the important role higher education has in uplifting the black community. For example, in his contribution to the *Colored American Magazine*'s series discussion, "Industrial Education—Will it Solve the Negro Problem?" Du Bois argued, "We believe that a rationally arranged college course of study for men and women able to pursue it is the best and only method of putting into the world Negroes with ability to use the social forces of their race so as to stamp out crime, strengthen the home, eliminate degenerates, and inspire and encourage the higher tendencies of the race not only in thought and aspiration, but in every-day toil."[15] Like Du Bois, Will believes that African Americans would benefit from receiving a liberal arts college education:

> He laughed at the idea of Latin and Greek being above the caliber of the Negro and likely to unfit him for the business of bread-getting in the peculiar position in life to which the Negro, as maintained by some, was destined from the beginning. . . . The only way to bring the best faculties of the Negro to their full fruition, he contended, was by the careful education of the moral faculties along the lines of

the natural laws. No Negro college, he argued, ought to bestow a diploma upon man or woman who had not been thoroughly grounded in the rudiments of moral and natural philosophy, physiology, and political economy. (167–68)

Hence, Will intends to serve his race as an educator, and as the novel concludes, he and Sappho plan to establish a school for young black intellectuals.

This characterization of Will Smith, especially when juxtaposed with Dr. Lewis and John Langley, has led some scholars to surmise that by 1899, Hopkins had chosen which side of the Washington–Du Bois debate to stand on. Barbara McCaskill, for example, claims that both Anna Julia Cooper and Hopkins were "staunch allies of Du Bois."[16] It is interesting to note that Hopkins manages to remain relatively neutral in *Contending Forces* on the specific question of the most appropriate form of institutional education for blacks in the sense that both Dr. Lewis's and Will Smith's plans for their schools receive equal attention, and there is no indication that either venture is or will be unsuccessful. Still, it is evident that the industrial and agricultural model is deemed a little less favorable, not because of the curriculum itself, but because Dr. Lewis "had been forced to compromise, and the educational advantages allowed the pupils had been curtailed to suit the views of those who placed a low estimate on the ability of the Negro" (288). The rivalry between these two leaders has become so well-known that we tend to read *Contending Forces* as a depiction of the tension. Yet it would be more accurate to recognize that Hopkins is foreshadowing if not predicting what would *later* escalate into an antagonistic relationship between these two men. By the time Hopkins had completed this novel, Washington was a household name. It would be another three years, however, before Du Bois would publish *The Souls of Black Folk*, with its compelling chapter "Of Mr. Booker T. Washington and Others," which would garner him national attention and notoriety. Prior to 1903, Du Bois, although recognized for his academic and intellectual gifts, was still making a name for himself. As a Cambridge resident, Hopkins likely knew of Du Bois's academic accomplishments, and had opportunities to hear his lectures when he visited Boston. It is probable that as a member of the Colored National League, Hopkins heard Du Bois's March 1901 address, "Does Education Pay?" in which he argued in favor of the liberal arts model of college education.[17] I suspect that Hopkins used this address and Du Bois's few early pamphlets to draw on when developing Will's character.

Hopkins uses the occasion of a protest meeting to bring these men together and present their perspectives on the key to overcoming the dehumanizing effects of racism and prejudice in order to achieve success in the

United States. The public Washington persona, Dr. Lewis, establishes a conciliatory tone when he addresses the audience at the rally by agreeing with points previously offered by the white conservative politician, Herbert Clapp. Northern protests, Dr. Lewis says, make life for southern blacks more difficult. During the remainder of Dr. Lewis's speech he echoes much of Washington's own attitudes. For example, Lewis states that blacks should eschew politics and "let matters of government take care of themselves, while we look out for our own individual or collective advancement, [and] find no difficulty in living at the South in peace and harmony with our neighbors. If we are patient, docile, [and] harmless, we may expect to see that prosperity for which we long, in the years to come, if not for ourselves then for our children" (250). In his Atlanta Exposition Address, Washington shuns politics as an area where blacks "began at the top instead of at the bottom."[18] "The wisest among my race," Washington claimed, "understand that the agitation of questions of social equality is the extremest folly, and that progress in the enjoyment of all the privileges that will come to us must be the result of severe and constant struggle rather than artificial forcing."[19] When Dr. Lewis says, "Convince the South that we do not want social equality, neither do we wish to rule" (251), he duplicates the same sentiment Washington expressed when he said "In all things that are purely social we can be as separate as the fingers."[20] Lewis receives a mixed reaction from the crowd, "murmurs of applause, mingled with disapprobation" and the narrator characterizes Dr. Lewis's address as "an eulogy" (251). The private Washington persona, Langley, addresses the audience next, and also expresses Bookerite sentiment when he states he does not "harbor undue resentment for the grievous wrongs which I feel [southern whites] have, in some measure, heaped upon us" (252). Langley discourages the audience from protesting the recent lynchings, and instead he encourages them to avoid antagonizing whites and upsetting the status quo: "Let us not offend the class upon whom we depend for employment and assistance in times of emergencies. By so doing, if we cannot have amity we can have peace" (253). He had previously promised to Clapp that he would keep the meeting "to a calm level" in exchange for a political appointment, which suggests that Hopkins had her suspicions of Booker T. Washington's true motivation behind his conciliatory manner (238).

Will Smith is the last to address the audience and receives the warmest reception. He confronts issues such as social assimilation ("miscegenation"), education, and politics, arguing that blacks need to be as politically active as Irish Americans, but that the vote alone will not solve the "Negro question." In terms of black education, Smith says that education alone will not remedy the problem of disenfranchisement even though he observes that blacks will be well-served by a thorough education, for it is "of the highest importance in the formation of the character of the individual, the race, the government, the social life of any community under heaven" (268). To solve the "Negro question," "Brute force will not accomplish anything. We must *agitate*" (272). If blacks can succeed in swaying public opinion to see the injustices perpetuated against them, Will believes, the country will become more enlightened and inclined to recognize the civil rights of African Americans. This protest rally, then, showcases Hopkins's astute understanding of not only where the Washington–Du Bois debate was heading, but also the challenges African Americans faced in sorting through advice from within the black community on making progress and succeeding as both individuals and as a community.

According to Brown, "Despite her impressive genealogy and the central role that her New England ancestors had played as abolitionists, educators, and activists on the international stage, she had remained on the margins of Boston's professional and social elite."[21] Nonetheless, I think Hopkins's ability to render these different points of view so adeptly as early as 1899 indicates the dynamic vantage point and foresight she held as a black intellectual at the turn of the century. It was this vantage point and foresight that Hopkins would draw on to offer her black readership a poignant translation of the gospel of success. By the time Hopkins joined the *Colored American Magazine* staff in 1900, she had a keen understanding of Washington's political rhetoric and the positions taken by his emerging opponents. According to Abby Johnson and Ronald Johnson, "The rivalry between accommodationist and radical approaches to race relations, between Booker T. Washington and W. E. B. Du Bois, climaxed in the first decade of the twentieth century. Nowhere did the controversy appear more clearly and dramatically than in contemporary Afro-American journals."[22] The *Colored American Magazine* was one such journal that became entangled in the controversy. When the *Colored American Magazine* was first published, the editorial board seemed ambivalent or, at best, lukewarm about Washington's leadership. In May 1900, the editors stated that they were proud to produce a magazine "devoted to the higher culture of Religion, Literature, Science, Music and Art of the Negro, universally."[23] This type of material was targeted at a middle-class audience that may not have agreed with Washington's pragmatism. The editorial board continued to outline its agenda in the "Editorial and Publisher's Announcements" for this same May issue. In it the editors proposed that the *Colored American Magazine* would fill the void left by white monthly magazines that had neglected "to sufficiently recognize our efforts, hopes and aspirations": "The *Colored American Magazine* proposes to meet this want, and to offer the colored people of the United States a medium through which they can demonstrate their ability and tastes, in fiction, poetry, and art, as well as in the arena of historical, social and economic literature. Above all it aspires to develop and intensify the bonds of that racial brotherhood, which alone can enable a people, to assert their racial rights as men, and demand their privileges as citizens."[24] Promoting racial solidarity was a key goal, not as an end in itself, but as a means of achieving justice and civil rights. Furthermore, this editorial condemned the South for its determination "to smile upon the servile, fawning, cowardly and sicko fantine [sic] negro and to frown upon the brave, manly, and aggressive negro."[25] These statements, plus the board's demand for justice, reflect a rather radical position.

But, ironically, in the next section of the announcements, the editors offered some support for Booker T. Washington, who by 1900 had developed a reputation for his conciliatory practices:

> Much has been said about Mr. Washington's plans or methods in conducting his school. His plans may not be yours, but I believe, if they reach the many poor boys and girls in many different sections of the South, you nor I should take exceptions to them. Complaint has often been made that he caters too much to the opposite race at the expense of his own, but we have failed, in a careful examination of everything that we have read, to discover any expression or sentence that would, in any way, convey such a thought in any of his addresses. . . . Surely whatever else he deserves, he does not deserve censure, criticism and calumny.[26]

It is not clear who authored this unsigned editorial. At the time, the editorial board consisted of ambitious black men, including Walter Wallace, managing editor; Peter Gilson, soliciting agent; H. S. Fortune, treasurer; Frederick F. Smith, advertising agent; Clarence J. Smith, corresponding editor; and J. Thomas Hewin, agent for Virginia. We can attribute it to one of the editors, perhaps Walter Wallace, the editor in chief in 1900, because he once wrote to Washington requesting financial assistance for the magazine. Historians have slightly different accounts of Hopkins's editorial involvement with the magazine. According to Ann Allen Shockley, Hopkins became the magazine's literary editor in November 1903.[27] Hazel Carby believes that Hopkins's editorial influence on the magazine has been underestimated, and she speculates that Hopkins took on the role of the magazine's editor before 1903, even though her name does not appear on the masthead until then.[28] Hopkins herself states that she was "engaged as literary editor" in May 1903 when the magazine was sold by its creditors.[29] Based on

Hopkins's negative depiction of Washington in *Contending Forces,* and the fact that in May 1900 she was a magazine contributor and did not become its literary editor until 1903, it is doubtful that she expressed this Bookerite sentiment. But clearly some members of the magazine staff felt the need to defend Washington. Many board members, including Wallace, were born in Virginia and moved to Boston in the 1890s. As transplanted southerners, they may have felt some affinity with one of the few southern blacks to achieve national prominence.

Why the ambivalence? Meier explains that many editors supported Washington's efforts because of the political climate and his control over the press, but they did not personally employ "his accommodating phraseology."[30] Many editors, in fact, "were sympathetic with his emphasis on economic accumulation and racial solidarity."[31] They had various motives for supporting Booker T. Washington within the pages of their publications. According to Meier, "A few editors perhaps agreed with his philosophy of accommodation. The majority were sympathetic with his emphasis on economic development as the basic solution to the race problem. . . . It should also be remembered that Washington's ascendancy coincided with the period of greatest oppression Negroes have faced since the Civil War. The resulting discouragement and frustration explain much of the instability in the ideologies of many individuals, and a great deal of the support Washington received."[32] Furthermore, some editors thought that Washington's accommodationist tactics were appropriate as long as they were used by southern, not northern, blacks.

By the time Hopkins emerged as literary editor in 1903, she had gradually distanced herself from those who felt the need to cultivate a relationship with Washington and she struggled to maintain an objective editorial position. Hopkins explained to William Monroe Trotter, a staunch anti-Bookerite and publisher of the *Boston Guardian,* that, "The new management maintained a respectful and conservative attitude towards Mr. Washington's policy, but held firmly to race fealty."[33] The magazine as a whole presented a balanced view to its readers, publishing and reprinting pieces by various writers both for and against Washington's policies and even pieces by Washington himself. For example, in "The Storm Before the Calm," a reprint of Washington's African Methodist Episcopal Church Conference address, Washington defended his program of industrial education for blacks, and he argued that blacks would earn their full citizenship not through "artificial forcing, but through the natural law of evolution."[34] Even though he believed it was an injustice for some whites to vote while blacks could not, Washington tried to convince this audience that blacks should take little interest in local politics and that he was against blacks participating in political agitation. An unsigned editorial printed in the same issue appears to respond directly to Washington's speech. The piece, entitled "The Negro: an Experiment," immediately follows an advertisement for *Contending Forces* and has a tone similar to Hopkins's other writings. Here the writer argued that the black vote, like black participation in party politics, was an experiment that blacks should pursue because they had little to lose and much to gain by it: "if in the meanwhile we are consummating and getting the molecules and atoms more closely connected by business meetings and racial contact, in years to come we will present such a stalwart phalanx of concentrated vim and manhood that it will take the combined efforts of all parties to keep us as a body from asserting ourselves manfully as citizens, and we will be heard."[35] Considering that Hopkins contributed a number of unsigned editorials to the magazine, it is not unlikely that she wrote this editorial. It is worth adding that often throughout the magazine, Hopkins's articles signed with one of her pseudonyms were placed adjacent to those signed with her real name to avoid giving readers the impression that her work dominated the magazine. For example, the September 1901 installment of her serialized novel *Hagar's Daughter*, printed under her pseudonym Sarah A. Allen (her mother's maiden name), immediately follows one of Hopkins's sketches in her "Famous Men of the Negro Race" series.[36] Nonetheless, several pages in the *Colored American Magazine* provide adequate proof of the second pseudonym. The "Editorial and Publisher's Announcements" for March 1902 revealed that Sarah A. Allen was the pen name Hopkins used for *Hagar's Daughter*.[37] An August 1902 advertisement attributed a forthcoming article, "Charles Winter Wood," to Sarah Allen (that is, Hopkins), but when the article was actually printed, it listed J. Shirley Shadrach as the author.[38] This key advertisement and article prove that Hopkins, Allen, and Shadrach were the same person.

As her tenure with the magazine continued, Hopkins became increasingly outspoken. She never attacked Washington by name, but she did criticize key aspects of his policy. She used articles like "Famous Men of the Negro Race" to conduct her own debate with Washington and his supporters, often inserting critical commentary at the end of a sketch that was directed at the Bookerites. In her biography of Robert Brown Elliott, for example, she offered an alternative definition of "industrial development": "The phrase 'industrial development' is greatly misunderstood by our white friends. To them it means an excuse, gladly hailed, to force the Negro to retrograde. To us it means, education of head and hand, not confining the Negro to any particular line of employment, with no intention of curtailing his efforts to raise himself into any business, profession or social condition that intrinsic worth and fitness may warrant him in seeking" (300). Unlike

Washington, who argued that "If we are poor, let us be poor," Hopkins did not want to impose any limits on black success.[39] This quoted selection refers to white readers, but she also implied that she was clarifying the meaning of industrial education for Washington, for he frequently solicited philanthropic support from whites and developed his industrial education model from Samuel Chapman Armstrong, principal of the Hampton Normal and Agricultural Institute and Washington's mentor. Washington believed economic success would help blacks achieve social and political success and asserted that "With economic development will come protection to property, security to life, and the right of trial by jury *in all cases*."[40] Yet, Hopkins believed that blacks could not devote all of their efforts to material gain and risk losing sight of the need for civil rights. In Lewis Hayden's sketch, she took the opportunity to comment, "Only by unintermitted [sic] agitation can a people be kept sufficiently awake to principle not to let liberty be smothered in material prosperity" (477). Furthermore, Hopkins's allusion to the biblical Judas in "Charles Lenox Remond" stopped just short of calling Washington a traitor of his race: "But what shall we say of the colored American who, having talent and opportunity to help build up, strengthen and succor us on our wearisome journey, deliberately adopts a policy of despair that will bind us down in a meaner bondage than that we have just escaped! For such a one there seems no atonement unless, like Judas of old, he be moved to acknowledge his sin and go out and hang himself" (38–39). Hopkins does not stop at merely hinting that Washington was being a traitor; in her "Famous Men" installment on Blanche K. Bruce, she used an incendiary quote from "the silver-tongued" Wendell Phillips to call southern whites "ignorant, embittered, [and] bedeviled" (261).

Interestingly, the last installment in Hopkins's "Famous Men" series, published in the October 1901 issue, is a sketch of Washington. Unlike the previous biographies, which seem motivated by a desire to educate and inspire the magazine's readers with accounts of past heroes, Washington's biography appears to be obligatory. It lacks detailed descriptions of heroics, courage, and generosity similar to those in the earlier "Famous Men" installments for Haitian Revolution leader Toussaint L'Ouverture (November 1900), Civil War veteran William Carney (June 1901), and politician Lewis Hayden (April 1901), respectively. The opening sentence of Washington's biography states, "The subject of this sketch is probably the most talked of Afro-American in the civilized world today, and the influence of his words and acts on the future history of the Negro race will be carefully acrutinized [sic] by future generations" (436). By beginning the article in this manner, Hopkins suggested that Washington had been chosen because of his current popularity, not necessarily because she believed his politics were best for the African American community. Taking into account Hopkins's acknowledgment that Washington occupied considerable space in discussions about race leadership, her extensive quotations from Washington's *The Story of My Life and Work* (1900) and her strategic silences about Washington's then-current political activities are conspicuous. In one sense, Washington's autobiography would prove useful for Hopkins's series on black success models, because in it he portrays himself as the black version of the Horatio Alger hero. According to Louis Harlan, both of Washington's 1900 and 1901 autobiographies "presented him to the world, not as the complex man that he privately was, but as the black version of the American success-hero and exemplar of the Puritan work-ethic he believed in."[41] On the one hand, Hopkins acknowledged the parallels between Washington's life and the lives of other self-made men: "Dr. Washington's early life and struggles are stories common to thousands of Negroes,—freedom, poverty, a desire for education, the hardships encountered to compass the coveted end, his admission to Hampton and his final graduation from that college . . . and his 'slumbering ambition' to become a lawyer" (436). On the other hand, Hopkins also called attention to some of Washington's complexities when she criticized some aspects of his uplift program. For example, she quoted his observation about how his Tuskegee students were initially opposed to manual labor and how they came to Tuskegee assuming they could avoid it by obtaining a college education. Then, she defended these students by adding, "We can well believe this prejudice against labor was true of the Negro, and we ought to expect nothing different from a class so long accustomed to see naught but excellence in the behavior of the white race. 'Massa Charles' lolled in his hammock while the slave worked. All the training of the Negro was in the direction that despised labor and made it a crime for a gentleman to labor" (437). This is a bold statement for Hopkins to make considering that she probably knew about Washington's position on not holding former slaveholders accountable for the current condition of African Americans.

Furthermore, Hopkins referred to Washington's Atlanta Exposition Address of 1895 as "his great speech," and she noted that he received "many flattering encomiums from leading men all over the country," but she did not comment on the speech's impact on the African American community. Instead, she characterized Washington's public speaking ability as entertaining: "Dr. Washington's public career as a speaker is full of interest. . . . His speeches on the Negro problem, and in behalf of the Institute, are able and teem with humor, and they possess also the essential property of attracting the attention of the monied element, for Dr. Washington is without a peer in this particular line, and as a result Tuskegee is the richest Negro educational plant in the world" (439). Hopkins also quoted from Washington's open letter to the South in which, by appealing to southerners' desire to attend to the protection of African Americans without northern interference, he urged them to stop the rash of lynching. Then, she criticized this conciliatory tactic: "It is all very well to talk of the Negro's immorality and illiteracy, and that raising him out of the Slough of Despond will benefit the South and remove unpleasantness between the races, but until the same course is pursued with the immoral and illiterate *white* Southerner that is pursued with the Negro, there will be no peace in that section. . . . The South keeps on in her mad carnage of blood: she refuses to be conciliated" (440). Hopkins continued her critique of Washington by comparing his response to the lynchings with that of abolitionist Quincy Ewing: "We hear a lot of talk against the methods of the antislavery leaders, but no abolitionist ever used stronger language than the Rev. Quincy Ewing of Mississippi, in his recent great speech against lynching. . . . The reverend gentleman does not believe in treating a cancer with rose water" (440). Hopkins wrote the following final assessment of the rise of Washington and Tuskegee Institute: "View his career in whatever light we may, be we for or against his theories, his personality is striking, his life uncommon, and the magnetic influence which radiates from him in all direction, bending and swaying great minds and pointing the ultimate conclusion of colossal schemes as the wind the leaves of the trees, is stupendous. When the happenings of the Twentieth Century have become matters of history, Dr. Washington's motives will be open to as many constructions and discussions as are those of Napoleon today, or of other men of extraordinary ability, whether for good or evil, who have had like phenomenal careers" (441). In short, she acknowledged his broad influence but also questioned his motives and practices.

There are other instances where it appears that Hopkins responded directly to Washington's articles and criticized his adaptation of the gospel of success. In September 1902, Washington's essay "Negro Homes" was reprinted in the magazine. In this article, Washington argued that the best way to determine the amount of progress blacks had made was to visit "the homes of the race." Washington described a Mississippi home he was a guest in, using language to depict the conservatively decorated house "as one would expect to find in Massachusetts."[42] The home had a parlor with reading material and a separate dining room, along with comfortable beds and clean bathrooms. Washington expressed his satisfaction that each member of the household exhibited race pride, and none were "ashamed of his people or wanted to discard the race to which Providence had assigned him."[43] In this piece Washington stressed the importance of property acquisition in the progress of the African American community. One of Hopkins's articles that appears later in the same issue speaks to Washington's emphasis on material gain as a sign of progress. In "Rev. John Henry Dorsey," Hopkins, using her pen name J. Shirley Shadrach, began the article by discussing the ordination of a black Catholic priest, the second black man in the United States to be ordained by the Roman Catholic Church. She used Dorsey as a springboard to launch into a discussion about the African American's moral virtues and aptitude for religious service. Here she also took a different perspective on the race's home environment, arguing that, "The Negro is true to his environment; he is no better and no worse than those whose conduct he copies in living, dress, education, religion and morals" (415). Thus, unlike Washington, who applauded blacks for emulating white standards of living, Hopkins argued that whites were no more virtuous than blacks, if not less so, and should hardly be used as a standard to measure progress. She offered an alternative view of the effect the pursuit of material gain was having on the African American community:

> But in politics it is the dollar that is against us as it is in everything—fraud, bribery, corruption, have destroyed principle.
>
> The Negro, too, has been bullied until he is gradually submitting to all indignities for the sake of a dishonorable peace and the almighty dollar.
>
> Mammon leads them on. (415–16)

Furthermore, in her November 1902 editorial, "Munroe Rogers," Hopkins criticized the black community's allegiance to the Republican Party: "No neither politics nor statesmanship can help the black man. The present administration has failed, previous administrations have failed because the Negro question is one of ethics too high for either party to grasp" (21). Her solution to this problem was a call for revolution:

> The fight is on; neither by the eloquence of the South nor by the wealth of Republicanism can the government hope to escape the iron hand of Destiny, whose fingers relentlessly manipulate the mill machinery of a just God.
>
> *Not* [sic] *agitate!*
>
> Republics exist only on the tenure of being constantly agitated. We cannot live without the voice crying in the wilderness—troubling the waters that there may be health in the flow. (26)

Finally, in "Latest Phases of the Race Problem in America," writing as Sarah A. Allen, Hopkins militantly argued that African Americans were entitled to the franchise: "We are told that the elective franchise is not a right, but a privilege. This is not true. In a government of the people, the elective franchise is an actual, absolute right,—a right belonging to every citizen who is free from crime. Any proposal to submit the question of the political or civil rights of the Negro to the arbitrament of the whites is as absurd as to submit the question of the political rights of the whites to the arbitrament of the Negroes, with one difference,—the Negroes are loyal to the Government" (245). In terms of the government, Hopkins discussed President Roosevelt's various political appointments and was skeptical of the outcome and of Roosevelt's intentions. She acknowledged that Roosevelt's black appointments had been benign, but she stopped short of trusting him completely. Considering Washington's political relationship with Roosevelt, and that he was known for advising him on appointments, Hopkins managed to attack Washington again without naming him specifically.

These later editorials help explain why Washington would have wanted Hopkins removed from her influential position at the magazine. Hopkins criticized the black community's allegiance to the Republican Party and refused to accommodate whites. According to Hazel Carby, Hopkins believed that "it was the duty of Northern black intellectuals like herself to revive a neglected New England tradition of radical politics."[44] In addition, Hopkins used her position on the editorial board to select and publish a particular brand of fiction in the magazine. Carby observes that "Hopkins regarded fiction as a particularly effective vehicle of instrumentation as well as entertainment. Fiction, Hopkins thought, could reach the many classes of citizens who never read history or biography."[45] Hopkins's privileging of fiction demonstrates the variety of forms "radical politics" assumed during this period. When control of the magazine, weakened by financial instability, changed to Booker T. Washington's hands in 1904, the emphasis of the articles shifted from literature and culture to politics and business. Although scholars know that the magazine's parent company, the Colored Co-Operative Publishing Company, began to suffer serious financial difficulties in 1903 and 1904, in actuality, it was suffering earlier than that. In August 1901, Walter Wallace, the Colored Co-Operative's founder and president, wrote to Booker T. Washington requesting financial assistance. Wallace explained to Washington that the company was in debt for one thousand dollars, for "it has always been self sustaining but through the ill advice of a party who has had fifteen years experience in the publishing business, we have dabbled in the publishing of books (an expensive luxury) from the surplus proceeds of the magazine to such an extent that we find the summer dullness upon us with no sinking fund to meet increased expense."[46] It is not clear if anyone else working on the magazine knew of the company's financial difficulties, for Wallace told Washington, "To the public, with our finely apportioned offices, surroundings, etc. it appears as a Gibraltar of strength."[47] It appears that Wallace did not inform Hopkins or the other staff members that he was going to appeal to Washington or if he received any financial support from the race leader, for in this letter Wallace assured Washington that all correspondence regarding the matter would be "strictly confidential." Years later, Washington admitted to owning some Colored Co-Operative stock certificates worth fifty dollars, "which I purchased simply for the purpose of helping the magazine out when it was in Boston," but he claimed that he disposed of the stock "as soon as I saw the assertion made that I was trying to control publications with money."[48]

A number of scholars have since written about Washington's attempts to influence the *Colored American Magazine* and his eventual takeover of the publication. William Stanley Braithwaite was the first to publish information about Washington's connection to the magazine, stating that by the time Frederick Moore was in charge, "It was now openly known that . . . the Colored American Magazine . . . under the management of Fred R. Moore, [was] controlled by Booker T. Washington."[49] August Meier's previously cited article, "Booker T. Washington and the Negro Press," uses Washington's correspondence to prove that he advised Moore on how to conduct and operate the magazine. Abby Johnson and Ronald Johnson, in their previously cited article, "Away from Accommodation," argue that Washington's intervention forced Hopkins off the magazine. Correspondence between Hopkins, William Monroe Trotter, and John C. Freund—that for some time had been presumed lost—provides additional insight into what happened to Hopkins and how her relationship with the magazine was severed.

As early as August 1904, just three months after Frederick Moore purchased the *Colored American Magazine*, Austin N. Jenkins, a partner in the Hertel, Jenkins and Co. publishing firm, privately accused Washington of owning the magazine and sending John C. Freund to advise the editors.[50] Washington denied any direct involvement with the magazine, but in January 1905 Du Bois made public accusations in the *Voice of the Negro* that editors of various black journals were allowing themselves to compromise their principles in exchange for a subsidy from Washington.[51] Du Bois was asked to substantiate this accusation when Oswald Garrison Villard, the editor of the *New York Evening Post* and a Tuskegee Institute benefactor, asked for the facts in February 1905 and again in March 1905.[52] In addition, William Hayes Ward, editor of the *Independent*, hinted that Du Bois's claims were slanderous.[53] Du Bois shied away from making additional accusations in the press, because he did not want to "wash our dirty linen in public."[54] Still, after being pressured to qualify his statements, on March 15, 1905, he wrote to William Monroe Trotter, editor of the *Boston Guardian*, for evidence: "Please send me by return mail every scrap of evidence you have going to prove Washington's bribery of newspapers. Send me as many documents as possible, references to documents, illustrative facts & sources for further knowledge & information. I want this for the private conversion of an influential man. . . . Give me *facts* & hurry them to me. Send a part at a time if necessary" (Du Bois's emphasis).[55] Trotter immediately complied with Du Bois's request: "I have sent one or two things more to-night. To-morrow I shall send you all the evidence I can find. It is necessarily of a circumstantial nature. . . . Would to God I had the direct evidence. But we may get that yet."[56] Du Bois, in turn, wrote to Villard on March 24, 1905, with his evidence.[57] Apparently, Trotter solicited information from Hopkins, but she was not able to reply as soon as he needed her to, for her account is not included in Du Bois's letter to Villard. But on April 16, 1905, one month after Du Bois requested information from Trotter, Hopkins sent Trotter her firsthand account of her experiences with the magazine and Washington's agents. She wrote Trotter a ten-page missive and attached approximately twenty-seven additional pages of supporting documentation. Evidently, Du Bois did eventually receive a copy of Hopkins's letter, for he quoted advice she received from John C. Freund, *word for word*, in his 1912 article, "The Colored Magazine in America": "As a white friend said: 'If you are going to take up the wrongs of your race then you must depend for support absolutely upon your race. For the colored man to-day to attempt to stand up to fight would be like a canary bird facing a bulldog, and an angry one at that.'"[58] This exact same passage is contained on page four of Hopkins's letter to Trotter. Hopkins herself was quoting a letter Freund sent to her on April 7, 1904.[59]

From the outset of Hopkins's letter to Trotter, she established that she had been and continued to be mistreated by Washington: "I have held these facts for a year, but as my rights are ignored in my own property, and I am persistently hedged about by the revengeful tactics of Mr. Washington's men, I feel that I must ask the advice of some one who will give me a respectful hearing."[60] According to Hopkins, the magazine was suffering from financial difficulty when it was sold to William H. Dupree, William West, and Jesse Watkins in May 1903. To solicit material for the magazine, Dupree approached John C. Freund, editor of a number of musical trade journals including *American Musician,* in the fall of that year and asked him for permission to reprint his series of articles on Jamaica. Not only did Freund grant permission, but he also provided financial assistance so the magazine could reproduce pictures to accompany the article. Freund, who was white, considered this an act of philanthropy: "I am very much interested in the colored people; indeed, I have a great regard for them, and anything I can do to be of service to them will always be done cheerfully, and to the best of my ability. I subscribe to one or two of the colored educational establishments in the South, and only wish I could do more than I am doing."[61] It is not clear if Hopkins and Dupree realized at that time that Freund might have been a supporter of the Tuskegee Institute. But in January 1904, Freund became more involved with the magazine by volunteering to hold a dinner for twenty of the city's black leaders to help further the interest of the magazine. This dinner took place on January 24, 1904, and the Colored American League was established, according to Freund, with "no political purpose whatever, but whose one aim shall be to encourage virtue, industry and patience among the colored people."[62] To that end, the *Colored American Magazine* would serve to facilitate the League's work. Hopkins told Trotter that after this meeting, "Mr. Freund took hold of our business ostensibly to correct our errors made in ignorance of the needs of a successful publication." Freund insisted that the price of the magazine be reduced from fifteen to ten cents an issue, but he made up the difference in revenue with private donations.[63]

By February 1904, Freund was also bestowing Hopkins with various presents, including flowers, furs, and books. The appropriateness of these personal gifts from a white man to a black woman was highly questionable, and Hopkins knew this. Freund's attention made Hopkins uncomfortable, but she continued her business relationship with him for the sake of the magazine. She explained to Trotter, "as I am not a woman who attracts the attention of the opposite sex in any way, Mr. Freund's philanthropy with regard to myself puzzled me, but knowing that he was aware of my burdens at home, I thought that he was trying to help me in his way. I was so dense that I did not for a moment suspect that I was being politely bribed to give up my race work and principles and adopt the plans of the South for the domination of the Blacks."[64] Soon Freund's political agenda was clear; he was a Bookerite who was against any presence of political agitation in the magazine. He wrote frequently to Dupree and Hopkins discouraging them from tackling race issues lest they antagonize potential white benefactors. In one letter to Dupree, Freud admonished, "I have also written to Miss Hopkins urging her to do her utmost to keep out of the magazine anything that might be construed into antagonism to the whites. We must take high ground in order to disarm opposition and bring out the good will of the white people who are not only with you now, but have always been with you only you have not known it."[65] Hopkins disclosed to Trotter that at one point Freund told her, "there must not be a word on lynching, no mention of our wrongs as a race, nothing that would be offensive to the South."[66] In addition, Freund was against the inclusion of editorials, essays, and literature in the magazine. He wrote to Hopkins, "To supply the colored people with literary matter is, in the best event, a thankless task." Freund believed that the magazine should be used to publish newsworthy material that would inform white audiences of the African American's progress, not "glittering generalities."[67] Ironically, Freund apparently did not read earlier issues of the *Colored American Magazine*; if he had, he would have seen that the periodical printed a variety of pieces, both literary and "practical." It is not clear if Hopkins spoke directly to Freund about his demands. But she definitely resisted his "advice," for the tone of Freund's letters is marked with frustration over Hopkins's and Dupree's apparent unwillingness to alter the editorial policy of the magazine. For example, on March 31, 1904, Freund explained to Dupree, "What we want is a magazine which shall devote itself not to essays, political arguments, but to a record of the work being done by the best class of colored people. You must lay down the law to Miss Hopkins, West and Watkins on this point. I have again and again endeavored to impress Miss Hopkins with this view, but she doesn't seem to grasp it."[68] Freund's direction that Dupree "lay down the law" that he himself had attempted repeatedly to "impress" upon Hopkins indicates Hopkins stood firm on her agenda. The following month Freund wrote to Dupree:

> There is, however, one rock right squarely ahead of us. That is the persistence with which matter is put into the magazine, which has no live interest, and furthermore, is likely to alienate the very friends who might help us. Now, I have spoke of the subject already more than I care to. Either Miss Hopkins will follow our suggestion in this matter . . . eliminating anything which may create offence; stop talking about wrongs and a proscribed race, or you must count me out absolutely from this day forth. . . . Every person that I have spoken on this subject is with me. IT IS MR. BOOKER WASHINGTON'S IDEA. If you people, therefore, want to get out a literary magazine . . . I refuse to work one minute longer with you. That is my ultimatum and I shall say no more on the subject.[69]

On the one hand, Hopkins may have curtailed criticism of Washington printed under her own name. On the other hand, she was more rebellious in articles signed with her pen name. One of the last essays she published in the magazine, "Mr. M. Hamilton Hodges" (March 1904), is signed Sarah A. Allen. Here, Hopkins wrote an article about a black musician implying that black musicians, and artists in general, could make a significant contribution to the struggle for equality. In other pieces, she slipped in comments as if she were having a debate with Freund and Washington. For example, despite Freund's February 1904 admonishments not to include literature in the magazine, the "Publisher's Announcements" for April 1904 quipped:

"That our readers are well pleased with our latest efforts to improve our publication and give them the best in the *literature and art* of the race, *is proven by the countless letters of commendation received*" (emphasis added).[70]

According to Hopkins, Freund continued to reveal more of "his true errand," which was to conduct a "Washington campaign." Freund decided that the *Colored American Magazine* needed Washington's support, and he insisted that Hopkins write a letter of introduction for him to present to Washington. Hopkins admitted to Trotter that she wrote this letter, even though she had no personal acquaintance with Washington.[71] Freund did meet with Washington in March 1904 and gained an ally, for Washington agreed with Freund on the proper content of the magazine: "Mr. Washington and I are absolutely agreed on this main point, that such a magazine as you have can be made a success, that is, that there is a demand for it among the whites as well as the colored people, but the magazine today is not what it should be because its conductors are sending it into a direction in which there is little or no interest—to produce a literary monthly which seems to be the controlling idea, will have absolutely no influence with your people or with the whites. For my part, I would not cross the street to buy what is called a 'literary monthly.'"[72] By early April 1904, Freund was threatening to withdraw his support from the magazine if Dupree and Hopkins did not cease and desist publishing what he considered to be incendiary material. Hopkins told Trotter that Freund's threats "threw a firebrand into the office and made my position unbearable." Surely Hopkins's colleagues did not want to risk losing major financial support from this benefactor. Yet Hopkins insisted on her course of action because she promised to publish certain pieces and she knew the readers would be disappointed if they were removed from the magazine. Evidently, in mid-April 1904, when Freund realized he would not succeed in dictating the magazine's editorial policy, he gave up in frustration: "I appear to have reached a point where my usefulness to you all has ceased, and my advice as to the policy is so distinctly in opposition to what you and [Dupree] believe to be the best for the enterprise, that no other course remains for me but to withdraw entirely from further participation."[73] As Freund exited, stage left, Washington entered, stage right, and purchased the magazine through Frederick Moore in May 1904. By June 1904 the magazine's office was moved to New York, and by September 1904 Hopkins was "forced out" to make room for Roscoe Conkling Simmons, Washington's nephew.[74]

There should be little ambiguity now about the cause of Hopkins's departure from the publication that was so instrumental in her writing career. Clearly Hopkins's defiant editorials and editorial policy put Booker T. Washington on the defensive. Purchasing the *Colored American Magazine* and moving its office from Boston to New York were the only effective means of silencing Hopkins. Although little documentary evidence exists to chronicle Pauline Hopkins's personal or professional relationships with contemporary black leaders and intellectuals of her era, her own writing reveals how involved and engaged she was with the debates about individual African American success and race progress. Not only does her work on self-made men maintain a high degree of currency, but it also demonstrates foresight that other black success writers were not able to sustain. As we shall see in the following chapter, Hopkins continued her outspoken critique of the gospel of success in her fictional depictions of African American life.

CHAPTER 3

"Mammon Leads Them On": Hopkins's Visionary Critique of the Gospel of Success

There is a stark difference between the real men in Pauline Hopkins's magazine articles and the male protagonists in her musical drama, short stories, and novels—between her nonfictional and fictional treatments of the success archetype. While her real-life self-made men are all successful, the majority of her fictional heroes either fail to reach the top rung of the success ladder, or else they must emigrate from the United States to fully realize their potential for financial achievement and social progress. In the biographical articles, Hopkins does not discourage her readers from trying to be successful. Rather, these articles have a didactic quality and suggest through examples of accomplished men how to climb the ladder of success while maintaining one's virtue and good character, and they define her standard of success for the African American community to place a stronger emphasis on making social contributions to one's own community. In short, her journalism advocates the application of the traditional success model—with significant modifications—to African American life. Yet, Hopkins's fiction explores the dynamics of the gospel of success differently than her nonfiction articles in the *Colored American Magazine* and *New Era Magazine*. Short stories like "General Washington, A Christmas Story" (1900) and "The Test of Manhood, A Christmas Story" (1902) portray young characters who fail to acquire or maintain social acceptance, wealth, and respectability. Hopkins's heroes in *Peculiar Sam, or The Underground Railroad* (1879), *Contending Forces* (1900), and *Of One Blood* (1902-1903), on the other hand, do become successful but do not experience it fully in the United States. By changing the conditions for which it is possible for African Americans to achieve success, Hopkins reveals the racism inherent in the American Dream and the negative impact racism has on the quality of life within the African American community.

Hazel Carby contends that, "Hopkins continued to write political fiction at the same time as she adopted popular fiction formulas and was the first Afro-American author to produce a black popular fiction that drew on the archetypes of dime novels and story papers."[1] Claudia Tate further speculates that reading Hopkins's fictional texts "probably incited pleasure" for her audience "because they enabled these readers temporarily to escape oppression and gain access to a collective racial desire for enlarged social opportunity as full-fledged American citizens."[2] One can seek "escape" by reading fiction, but I would argue that Hopkins sought to educate, not pacify her readership. Even as Hopkins acknowledged having "introduced [into *Contending Forces*] enough of the exquisitely droll humor peculiar to the Negro (a work like this would not be complete without it) to give a bright touch to an otherwise gruesome subject" her main objective in portraying lynching, mob violence, and sexual exploitation was "to raise the stigma of degradation from [her] race," hardly an escapist venture (16, 13). For Hopkins, popular literature for the African American masses offered more than a momentary reprieve from the severe reality of living during the nadir. In the now frequently quoted preface to *Contending Forces*, she wrote, "Fiction is of great value to any people as a preserver of manners and customs—religious, political and social. It is a record of growth and development from generation to generation," expressing her commitment to using popular fiction to document and motivate black people to achieve progress and to succeed in life (13-14). Hopkins's ability to craft her fiction in this way distinguished her from other African American success writers of the period who limited their discourse on success to nonfiction.

John Cawelti has examined the differences between fiction and nonfiction success literature and notes that both maintain the same plot formulation: a vulnerable (often orphaned) young hero struggles against adversity and moral temptation to achieve respectability and increased material wealth. But while in self-help handbooks and articles "industriousness, frugality, and piety are the operative factors in the hero's rise in society," novels attribute the hero's success to a good deed that he performs, his marriage to an heiress, or his being in the right place at the right time.[3] In other words, in success fiction "the hero's problems are solved by a kind of magic rather than by a clearly envisioned process of cause and effect."[4] Similarly, Hopkins promotes one set of values in her journalism—strong intellect, morality, and honor—and then subverts them in her fiction by depicting characters who possess these qualities but still fail to succeed. As Carby notes, Hopkins "believed that writing fiction was an especially effective means of intervening politically in the social order."[5] Even though Hopkins's fiction served as an avenue for her political expression, Carby reminds us that she still had to contend with reaching a wide readership. Thus, her objective was to "combine elements of popular fiction with a more didactic intent to create stories of political and social critique."[6] In Hopkins's fiction, a black man's possession of the right qualities alone cannot make him successful as long as racism and apathy obstruct his path to success. In Hopkins's short stories and novels, she undermines the American Dream by exposing the limited extent to which the traditional success archetype can be applied to African Americans. The formula plots of traditional success literature often read like predictable fairy tales that enable readers to anticipate the hero's actions and eventual triumph. As Kilmer explains, "Readers predict what will happen, and, in so doing, enjoy anticipating the triumph of virtue and the downfall of vice. The stock characters, the lexicon of actions and clichés, instill a sense of control over the random forces of evil."[7] Hopkins's work within this genre is distinctive because she takes popular tropes of the success plot and gives them a new, racialized significance for the purpose of illustrating the typical African American's lack of control over the evil forces of prejudice and discrimination that he often encounters in his day-to-day life. Once she establishes the trope, she abandons the predictable path by altering the outcome one would expect of stories that use these literary devices. In this manner she illustrates how United States racism can hinder an African American's ability to work his way from rags to respectability.

As noted above, success fiction generally follows a standard formula and a number of tropes are employed to chronicle the hero's adventures. First, in the traditional story the setting plays an important role in the hero's success and the urban street often represents hardship and poverty. As heroes change and improve their living accommodations from the sidewalk to a benefactor's home, they move closer to respectability. Clothing, a second trope, also changes and improves in relation to a character's perceived success. Third, coincidence and luck help make heroes more prosperous and allow them to reap the benefits of their hard work and determination. This hard work frequently takes the form of a brave act that puts the protagonist in a position to receive a benefactor's generosity. Furthermore, benevolent patrons reward heroic acts and supply the hero with clothing, money, a secure home, and gainful employment. In short, benefactors lead young boys to success. Her definition of success is similar to the paradigm she establishes in her magazine articles: success is defined as having risen from an impoverished or modest background to earn fame, social acceptance, and a moderate income. The main character's ultimate goal is to make significant contributions to his community and help lift up other African Americans. Yet, Hopkins's fictional heroes frequently fail in life despite changing environments or acquiring new clothing. Luck and coincidence often work against the young men, and white men who would have been their benefactors fail to support them because of their own racial prejudices. All of her heroes that do succeed do so by following a path that leads them out of the United States.

One of the best-known novels in the success literary genre is Horatio Alger's *Ragged Dick*, which was originally published as a serial in *Student and Schoolmate* in 1867.[8] Granted, the self-made man is not unique to Horatio Alger's novels, and as Cawelti acknowledges, "Alger neither created the Alger hero nor was he his only exponent, but Alger's protagonists are synonymous with the idea of the self-made man, and he outsold other success writers like Oliver Optic, Sarah Robbins and Elijah Kellog."[9] Alger's work is particularly useful to this study because of his focus on social mobility (instead of wealth or power), which aligns with Hopkins's version of success that emphasizes social respectability. Hopkins's fiction employs Alger's same tropes, yet with a difference.

Peculiar Sam; or The Underground Railroad appears to be Hopkins's earliest known treatment of the success myth. She wrote *Slaves Escape; or The Underground Railroad* sometime in 1879 and changed the name of the play to *Peculiar Sam* shortly thereafter. During the course of the play, Sam and the other characters take advantage of various opportunities to display their vocal talents and sing nostalgic songs about "Ol' Master" and slave cabins. One wonders why Hopkins chose to write a musical about slavery fourteen years *after* emancipation. Carby suggests that Hopkins is using this fictional history in this play to "provide her readers with an understanding of the source of contemporary forms of oppression."[10] But, it appears that Hopkins is trying to showcase the original lead singer, Sam Lucas, by incorporating songs from his standard repertoire into the musical. Hopkins's biographer, Lois Brown, believes "The speed with which *Underground Railroad* was showcased suggests that Hopkins was commissioned to write the piece," and she cites advertisements in the *Minneapolis Tribune* as evidence that Hopkins was "selected to create this musical drama."[11]

The play opens in the antebellum South. The protagonist, Sam, decides to help his mother, Mammy, his sister, Juno, and his sweetheart, Virginia, runaway after he learns that Virginia has been married to Jim, a black overseer, against her will. In Act I, Sam and the other characters discuss Virginia's fate in an old slave cabin. Virginia tells them she will run away rather than remain on the plantation and be forced into a loveless marriage as if she is a concubine. Although the subject of rape is not explicitly treated in this play, Virginia's chastity is in jeopardy and at the whims of white slaveholders. While I would not consider Virginia the protagonist, it is worth noting that her urgent need to leave the plantation parallels the traditional success hero's need to escape the street "where, if they remain, moral decay and poverty are certain."[12] In *Ragged Dick*, for example, Richard Hunter lives in a wooden box filled with straw on Spruce Street in New York City. He decides to rent a room at a boardinghouse at the same time that he realizes he has ambitions for improving his life: "So he determined to hunt up a room which he could occupy regularly, and consider as his own, where he could sleep nights, instead of depending on boxes and old wagons for a chance shelter. This would be the first step towards respectability, and Dick determined to take it" (58). Like Richard Hunter, Virginia and Sam decide that leaving their current environment will help them move closer to womanhood and manhood, respectively. Thus, Virginia states, "it's hard to leave the place where I was born, but it is better to do this, than to remain here, and become what they wish me to be. To fulfill this so-called marriage," while Sam declares, "Yes, we's all gwine to Canidy! Dars been suthin' a growin' an' a growin' inter me, an' it keep sayin,' 'Run 'way, run away, Sam. Be a man, be a free man.'"[13] Sam's family may have misconceptions about Canada, but they are convinced that living there would be better than where they are being forced to reside. Sam's sister Juno exclaims, "I know whar dat is, dar aint no slabe niggers dar, dey's all tooken care on by Mrs. Queen Victoria, she's de Presidunt ob Canidy" (105). Brown reads *Peculiar Sam* as a "play on black domesticity" where the slave cabin "becomes a refined signifier of the domesticity and humanity that the slaves possess in spite of their enslavement."[14] But if one reads the first act within the success paradigm, one observes that Hopkins establishes the fact that remaining in an American setting, on the plantation, would mean suffering for Virginia and Sam whereas Canada promises independence and happiness.

Many success writers have adverse feelings toward American cities. According to Richard Weiss, "While the city was a place of opportunity, it also was a place of unspeakable corruption and moral turpitude. Virtue resided in the country."[15] However, Hopkins uses the runaway slave motif to subvert the traditional privileging of rural America. In this play, Hopkins Signifies on the traditional trope by rendering the rural slave plantation as the locus of corruption and immorality. Sam reiterates the significance of the groups' journey when he tells Caesar, another African American character he encounters en route, "We're trablin' to Canidy. 'Deed uncle dey is gittin' so hi on des plantations dat a fellar's got to run 'way ef he's got eny 'spectible feelin's 'tall" (109). If Virginia and Sam remain, she surely will be forced to succumb to Jim's advances and Sam will be sold farther south, stripped of his masculinity, and unable to protect Virginia's virtue. Therefore, Hopkins delivers the characters safely to another country, implying that neither black womanhood nor black manhood are protected anywhere in the United States, North or South.

In the final act, all of the characters reunite on Christmas Eve in Mammy's Canadian home. Now that the slaves have escaped to Canada, it is safe for them to perform legitimate domestic activities without being victimized by a white slaveholder. Mammy sits knitting at her kitchen table and Caesar, now her husband, sits at the warm hearth and updates the audience on the family's progress: "Ol' 'ooman it are a long time sense we an' de chillern lef' de ol' home, seems to me de Lor' has blessed us all. Hyars you an' me married, Jinny a singist, Juno a school marm; an' las' but not leas,' dat pecoolar Sam, eddicated an' gwine to de United States Congress" (119). Thus, Caesar and Mammy's Canadian marriage, which juxtaposes the sham marriage between Virginia and Jim on the southern plantation, and Juno, Virginia and Sam's new professions are indicative of their success. Ironically enough, Mammy and Caesar miss being on the plantation even though they appear to be living comfortably in Canada. After Virginia's rendition of a song "after style of 'Swanee River,'" Mammy tells Caesar:

> Ol' man, Ise totable 'tented hyar till I hears dat dear chile sing dem ol' songs, in dat angel voice ob hers, an' den I feels so bad, kase dey carries me way bact to dem good ol' times dat'll neber return. De ol' plantation, an' Mistis an' ol' Marser, an' de dear little lily chillern; thar I kin seem to see de fiel's ob cotton, an' I kin seem to smell de orange blossoms dat growed on de trees down de carriage drive. (wipes her eyes) Ise been totable 'tented hyar, but I boun' to trabble back 'gin 'fo' I die.
>   CAESAR: (wiping his eyes) An' ol' 'ooman, ef de ol' man dies firs,' bury me at ol' Marser's feet, under de 'Nolin tree. (119)

If Hopkins's overall objective is to comment on the United States' failure to support the African American's dream of success, it is not clear what purpose these episodes of nostalgia serve. Perhaps Mammy and Caesar represent the older generation of slaves who have selective memories about the "good old days" on the slave plantation. Or, this episode serves to place the musical score within a certain cultural context. Indeed, the directions for the musical selections were loosely arranged, and at one point, Sam Lucas is instructed to introduce "any of his songs that have not been sung elsewhere" (121). The fact remains that Hopkins chooses to close the play with Sam dancing and the "remainder happy" *outside* the United States (123). Closing the play in Canada is consistent with the play's larger theme that blacks must leave the United States to fully realize success and progress.

In addition to locale, Hopkins employs another literary device of the traditional success formula, costume changes, throughout Sam's journey from southern slavery to northern freedom. The stage directions indicate that Sam first appears on stage dressed as a field hand (100). Although these directions are not specific, one can imagine Sam's attire is made of the dingy, coarse cloth commonly supplied to slaves during this time period. Later, as Sam prepares to run away from the plantation, he enters the scene "dressed as [a] gentleman overseer" (108) and his family does not recognize him. When they do, his sister says, "What a peccoliar fellar you is! Look jes like a gemman" (108). At first Hopkins seems less focused on promoting Sam's hidden virtues than she is on portraying his trickster side. In the traditional success tale, when the hero dresses up, the narrator or other characters comment on his improved appearance. In *Ragged Dick*, the narrator observes that once Richard cleans himself up, "He now looked quite handsome, and might readily have been taken for a young gentleman" (18). By cleaning up the hero's outward appearance, Alger attempts to make the boy's innate noble character believable. Sam's disguise, along with his travel pass that allows him and his family to attend a religious camp meeting, enables him to move freely from the oppressive plantation to the liberating Canadian border. He assumes another disguise as an "old man" just as he is about to leave the hideout and cross the river to Canada (117). On the surface Hopkins uses the dress changes as opportunities for the performers to showcase their singing abilities; the stage directions that accompany this scene indicate that Sam "Sings old man character songs, 'Old Man Jake'" (117). After Sam's final wardrobe change, his new attire reflects his improved social position as indicated by his new profession in the United States Congress. Sam enters Mammy's kitchen and "throws off wraps" (120). This cloak, along with new speech patterns, signals his improved class status to the audience.

In "General Washington, A Christmas Story" the hero's attempts to improve his attire and overall appearance do not result in the same type of success that Sam achieves. In fact, the General's appearance, specifically his brown skin that marks his racial identity, contributes to his downfall because of the racial and color prejudice that pervaded in the United States at the turn of the century. This short story chronicles the brief life of a child who sells chitlins on the streets and dances in bars to earn a living. From an early description of the General's home life one can assume that his clothing is poor: " . . . the child would drift from one squalid home to another wherever a woman—God save the mark!—would take pity upon the poor waif and throw him a few scraps of food for his starved stomach, or a rag of a shawl, apron or shirt, in winter, to wrap about his attenuated little body."[16] This orphan's clothes consist of "a wardrobe limited to a pair of pants originally made for a man, and tied about the ankles with strings, a shirt with one gallows, a vast amount of 'brass,' and a very, very small amount of nickel" (70). Hopkins's contemporary readers who were familiar with fictionalized success stories would recognize the parallels between the General's early wardrobe and that of the traditional archetype. In *Ragged Dick*, the hero is introduced to the reading audience wearing the tattered clothes that reflect his life as a street urchin: "Dick's appearance as he stood beside the box was rather peculiar. His pants were torn in several places, and had apparently belonged in the first instance to a boy two sizes larger than himself. He wore a vest, all the buttons of which were gone except two, out of which peeped a shirt which looked as if it had been worn a month. To complete his costume he wore a coat too long for him, dating back, if one might judge from its general appearance, to a remote antiquity" (4). Neither Dick nor the General's appearance is intended to be taken at face value, however. Beneath the General's dirty and tattered exterior is a sensitive child who rescues a stray kitten from some cruel, privileged children.

The General meets a young white girl named Fairy on the streets, and in typical Alger fashion, this encounter awakens the General's consciousness to his current lack of cleanliness and the opposing social statuses of the children. Dressed well in "costly velvet and furs," Fairy directs him to shake hands with her. He responds:

"Deed, missy, I'se 'tirely too dirty to tech dem clos o' yourn."
Nevertheless he put forth timidly and slowly a small paw begrimed with the dirt of the street. He looked at the hand and then at her, she looked at the hand and then at him. Then their eyes meeting, they laughed the sweet laugh of the free-masonry of childhood.
"I'll excuse you this time boy," said the fairy, graciously, "but you must remember that I wish you to wash your face and hands when you talk with me; and, . . . it would be well for you to keep them clean at other times, too." (74)

Fairy invites the General to her home on Christmas morning for religious instruction about God and salvation. In preparation for this house call, Hopkins notes that "Trade was good, and the General, mindful of the visit next day, had bought a pair of second-hand shoes and a new calico shirt" (77). In traditional success literature, new clothes signal pending improved circumstances for the hero. "The good suit, which is usually presented to the hero by his patron," Cawelti explains, marks the initial step in his advancement, his escape from the dirty and ragged classes and his entry upon respectability."[17] The fact that the General must acquire secondhand clothes on his own bespeaks of his want of a patron. Furthermore, unlike Alger's white heroes like Ragged Dick and Luke Larkin, who are trusted by benefactors and others because of honest faces, the General is received by Fairy's grandfather with suspicion when he goes to his house to warn him of a plot to rob his home. The Senator sees the General's skin color and responds to

"General Washington." From the December 1900 issue of the Colored American Magazine.

the General's presence by calling him a "black rascal," while accusing him of being a thief (80).

In Hopkins's texts, luck and coincidence are not used in the traditional sense, but often prove to be detrimental to the main characters instead. In "General Washington," the General happens to fall asleep under a table in Dutch Dan's bar. Hopkins writes, "He was lucky, he told himself sleepily, to have so warm a berth that cold night; and then his heart glowed as he thought of the morrow and Fairy, and wondered if what she had said were true" (78). This statement could be interpreted as a sign of good things to come. One would think that the General is lucky to be under the table and overhear Jim's plot to rob a house, which is, coincidently, Fairy's residence. Luck plays against him, however, when he goes to the Senator's home to warn him about the robbery and instead of receiving a monetary reward, he is confronted with suspicion. According to Kilmer, rags-to-riches plots usually include a point during which the hero wins his benefactor's respect through "an act of bravery made possible only by improbable coincidence."[18] Ragged Dick saves a drowning boy who falls off a ferry boat. The boy's father, Mr. Rockwell, rewards Dick for his heroic actions by supplying him with new clothes and giving him a job as a counting-room clerk in his firm. In another Alger novel, Luke Larkin bravely stands trial for a crime he did not commit, and in return for his honesty and good character, his benefactor, Roland Reed, rewards him with two new suits, a new watch, and a job doing collections. Reed tells Luke, "Do your duty, Luke, and your good fortune will continue."[19] In both cases, the reward is clear for the young white boys. Unlike the traditional success archetype, Hopkins's hero is not rewarded for his brave act. The General risks his life to warn the Senator of an impending robbery, but meets suspicion merely because of his race:

> "Please, boss, it hain't me, it's Jim the crook and de gang from Dutch Dan's." . . .
>
> It was ten minutes of the hour by the Senator's watch. He went to the telephone, rang up the captain of the nearest station, and told him the situation. He took a revolver from a drawer of his desk and advanced toward the waiting figure before the fire.
>
> "Come with me, keep right straight ahead through that door; if you attempt to run I'll shoot you." (80-81)

Instead of receiving new clothes and a new job, as one familiar with these types of stories would expect, the General faces the barrel of a gun pointed at him by a racist white man. Instead of being a benevolent patron, the Senator accosts the General, threatens him with violence, and does not protect him. In Hopkins's revised success fiction, black boys face suspicion from potential white benefactors. Even though the General displays honesty and good character like a typical Alger hero, he is murdered and the police take the credit for capturing Jim and his gang. Unlike Luke Larkin, who is rewarded for his work in helping to identify the true bank robber, the General is rewarded with violence. He is not even acknowledged for his role in the defeated robbery plot.

Although this is clearly not the happy ending that audiences come to expect, in some respects the General's brave act benefits the entire race. Race uplift and community self-help are significant facets of Hopkins's brand of African American success. By risking his own life to help someone else, the General displays the virtues that the Senator does not believe African Americans possess. His life is offered up as an example of the high moral character that exists in the black community. Still, it is not clear whether Hopkins intends the General's death to be positive or negative. She writes, "The General had obeyed the call of One whom the winds and waves of stormy human life obey. Buster's Christmas Day was spent in heaven. For some reason, Senator Tallman never made his great speech against the Negro" (82). On the one hand, the General fails to be justly rewarded during his lifetime for his efforts. Yet, on the other hand, his spirit ascends to heaven and his death influences the Senator enough to change his mind about African Americans. In these respects the General is a martyr and Hopkins sacrifices the General for the greater good of the African American community.

In "The Test of Manhood, A Christmas Story," Hopkins revisits the theme of traveling in search of a better life. Mark Myers, a young man from an unspecified southern town, makes a conscious decision to leave home and pass as a white man in a northern city. The reader is introduced to the hero just as he is "leaving his home to try his fortune at the North."[20] During his journey, he travels as if he is a fugitive: "He avoided the main roads and kept to the fields, thus keeping clear of all chance acquaintances who might interfere with his determination to identify himself with the white race" (206). It appears that Hopkins deliberately portrays the American South as a place that blacks need to escape from, instead of a rural haven of morality and virtue. Mark makes his way to Boston, where he finds work for a lawyer, attends night school, passes the bar exam, and eventually becomes engaged to his employer's daughter Katherine.

Traditionally, good deeds are rewarded by a benevolent patron who recognizes the adolescent's potential and steers him on the right path to success. Mark Myers arrives in Boston and almost immediately has the opportunity to earn a benefactor's respect. John Brown drops his wallet when he rushes past Mark on the street. Mark picks it up and finds Brown's card along with a large sum of money. At this point, Hopkins calls attention to Mark's strong ethical character: "Mark stood a second hesitating as to the right course to pursue; here was wealth—money for food, shelter, clothes—he sighed as he thought of what it would give him. But only for a moment, the next he was rushing along the wide mall at his utmost speed trying to overtake the gentleman whom he could just discern making his hurried way through the throng of pedestrians" (207). When Mark returns the wallet, Brown mistakes him for a white boy and offers him a monetary reward and a job: "now that was clever of you and very honest, my boy," says Brown (207). Readers have come to expect this type of reward, but Mark is not white and one wonders if he would have been rewarded as favorably if this fact had been known, or if Brown would have called the police and accused Mark of stealing the wallet, just as Senator Tallman accuses the General of breaking into his home.

Mark's comely appearance serves him well at Brown's firm. When Mark reports to work he presents himself neatly, and although his reading and writing skills are not as strong as his husbandry skills, Brown gives Mark a job anyway, noting that "I like your face, and your manner, too, my lad, and although it is contrary to my way of doing—taking a boy without a reference—because of your honesty you may set in as a porter and messenger here" (208). Possessing an honest face seems to work to Mark's advantage just as it does in standard success plots. For example, in Alger's *Struggling Upward*, Mr. Armstrong comments on Luke's wholesome appearance while discussing his acquittal for robbing a bank. Stating that he never would have suspected Luke of robbery, he adds, "I claim to be something of a judge of character and physiognomy, and your appearance is in your favor" (206).

Despite his honest face, luck and coincidence put Mark Myers at a disadvantage. Mark's mother, Aunt Cloty, comes to Boston in search of her son. When she falls ill and is unable to support herself as a laundress, she coincidentally becomes Katherine's charity case. Mark does not know that Aunt Cloty is in Boston, or that she and Katherine have become close until he encounters her at Katherine's home on Christmas Eve:

> As [Katherine] spoke she threw wide the doors and in the midst of the glitter and dazzle he heard a voice scream out:
> "Oh, my Gord! It's him! It's my boy! It's Sonny!" . . .
> After that scream came a deathly silence, Mark stood as if carved into stone, in an instant he saw his life in ruins, Katherine lost to him, chaos about the social fabric of his life. (217)

If this were a traditional success story, a happy family reunion would accompany the revelation of Aunt Cloty's and Mark's true identities. Nevertheless,

Hopkins puts a high price on such reunions. Because Mark has been passing for white, if he acknowledges his mother, he loses his wife-to-be, the support of Judge Brown, and his tentative partnership with Brown's law firm. Yet, for Hopkins, Mark's noble character is an important virtue for a successful man, and at the conclusion of the story, instead of rejecting his mother, he acknowledges her:

> He turned slowly and faced Judge Brown and there was defiance in his look. All that was noble in his nature spoke at last.
> Another instant his arms were about his fond old mother, while she sobbed her heart out on his breast. (217)

According to Cawelti, the hero's success does not owe to luck alone; he must be worthy of the success as evident in his virtues, especially character and intellect.[21] Hopkins initially depicts Mark's patron as the typical surrogate father figure of the success literary genre. He gives Mark his first job, and at the end of several years, he is prepared to make Mark a partner in his law firm, as well as give Mark his daughter's hand in marriage. Yet, when Mark reveals his true racial identity to Judge Brown and Katherine, the reader is left to question whether Mark will still be welcomed in the Judge's home and family. Instead of revealing a hero to be an heir, the protagonist's true identity works against him. In light of the social conditions for blacks in the early 1900s, one can assume that Mark will lose the success he has garnered in spite of his comely appearance and good deeds.

In the wake of absent benefactors, Hopkins uses her longer fiction to advocate for black people helping themselves and each other to succeed. In *Contending Forces*, Hopkins combines conventions of the romantic novel, historical novel, and success story to chronicle the lives of the Montfort family and their descendants, the Smiths, and their attempt to find happiness and prosperity. Even though most of the action in this novel occurs in the United States, particularly Boston, shifting environments play a role in the plot development. In the first part of the novel, Charles Montfort, a white Bermudan slaveholder, resolves to relocate his family and estate to the United States to avoid losing his fortune to impending British emancipation laws. Tragedy strikes in Newbern, North Carolina, when Montfort is murdered and his wife and children are beaten and remanded to slavery by Anson Pollock, a jealous rival. Montfort's wife Grace commits suicide rather than submit to being Pollock's slave and mistress. Montfort's son, Charles Jr., is sold to a British mineralogist, while his other son, Jesse, runs away when on an errand in New York. Once again Hopkins Signifies on the notion of moving up in the world by orchestrating Montfort's tragic loss after moving to the United States. Typically, immigrants come to the United States to secure better living conditions and wealth. But Hopkins does not allow the Montfort family to experience the American Dream as one would expect. Even though Montfort intends to free all of his slaves and retire to England, he chooses to reestablish his plantation in the American South, "where the institution flourished, and the people had not yet actually awakened to the folly and wickedness exemplified in the enslavement of their fellow-beings" (24). Montfort's friends try to dissuade him from leaving Bermuda, and characterize the United States as a wild, foreign nation. A clergyman warns Montfort, "They tell me that for all their boasted freedom, the liberty of England is not found, and human life is held cheaply in the eyes of men who are mere outlaws" (25-26). Clearly the cleric is foreshadowing Montfort's suffering in the South. Indeed, in the preface to the novel, Hopkins comments on the barbarity of the South: "'Rule or ruin' is the motto which is committing the most beautiful portion of our glorious country to a cruel revival of piratical methods; and, finally, to the introduction of *Anarchy*" (15). In *Contending Forces,* as in *Peculiar Sam* and "The Test of Manhood," Hopkins casts the American South as the wild "street" environment that heroes need to be rescued from. Furthermore, when Jesse runs away from Anson Pollock, his life improves. Jesse makes his way to the North, marries a black woman, and settles in Exeter, New Hampshire.

Henry Smith, Jesse's son-in-law, is an example of a self-made man. He migrates from Virginia at a young age and moves to New Bedford, Massachusetts, where "he had imbibed . . . an unwavering desire for all the blessings of liberty, and strong notions that a man must depend upon himself in great measure and carve out his own fortune to the best of his ability with such tools as God had furnished him" (82). Like many self-made men, he does not have a formal education, but he has "a naturally intelligent manner" (82). Henry spends some time working as a sailor before settling in Boston. Unfortunately, Boston is not the generous land of opportunity that readers are wont to assume. Even though one would expect a city like Boston to be more conducive to success, Hopkins chooses to depict the racism and job discrimination that many blacks face, and thus subverts the traditional trope of the northern city as the safe haven and promised land for blacks:

> The masses of the Negro race find for employment only the most laborious work at the scantiest remuneration. A man, though a skilled mechanic, has the door of the shop closed in his face here among the descendants of the liberty-loving Puritans. The foreign element who come to the shores of America soon learn that there is a class which is called its inferior, and will not work in this or that business

if "niggers" are hired; and the master or owner, being neither able nor willing to secure enough of the despised class to fill the places of the white laborers, acquiesces in the general demand, and the poor Negro finds himself banned in almost every kind of employment. (83)

Henry decides not to battle against the greater forces of prejudice, and establishes his own tailoring business instead. He dies before he can reach his full potential as a self-made entrepreneur. But, Henry passes the legacy of the success archetype on to his son, Will. In many respects, Will is characterized as a typical Horatio Alger hero who is fatherless and vulnerable. Henry's death leaves his wife, daughter, and son forced to support themselves and their heavily mortgaged house in Boston's South End. Will is preparing to go to college when his father dies, but he "cheerfully" gives up his plans to attend school and works as a bellboy in a local hotel to help support his family. Will's noble devotion to his family is very similar to Luke Larkin's, an Alger hero who works as his school's janitor to assist his widowed mother with their living expenses.

Throughout the novel, Will's attempts to raise himself up are portrayed in a secondary, but still significant, subplot. Will hopes to finish college and attend graduate school in Germany. He has already earned some notice for a few scholarly articles he has written, "and one wealthy gentleman had offered him a course at Heidelberg after graduation" (168). Still, Will does not perform heroic deeds that earn him a benefactor's esteem. Instead, Hopkins uses coincidence to ensure that Will and his eventual benefactor cross paths. Will is invited to a dinner at the Canterbury Club, where Charles Montfort-Withington, a member of the British Parliament, is a guest. Withington turns out to be Ma Smith's first cousin, and with his help, the Smith family's true identity is established. The family's estate, one hundred and fifty thousand dollars, is restored to them by the United States government. The Smith family's success is not quite the fulfillment of the American Dream, however. Although the United States Supreme Court provides Will and his family with wealth, the American legal system is merely reinstating the fortune that was first established in Bermuda. Furthermore, this windfall is made possible primarily with a British citizen's help. Ultimately, the United States has little to do with Will's success. He earns several honors overseas, and cultivates the bearing "of a man accustomed to the respectful attention of his equals, sure of himself, his position, his attainments—a wealthy cosmopolitan" (385). Hopkins makes a point of noting that Will matures into an accomplished race leader beyond the borders of the United States.

Like the many subjects of Hopkins's "Famous Men" series, Will is dedicated to serving others: "The ambition of his life was the establishment of a school which should embrace every known department of science, where the Negro youth of ability and genius could enter without money and without price. This was his pet scheme for the future . . . he would be a father to the youth of his race" (386). When Will visits Dora and Dr. Lewis in New Orleans, he suggests that they move their school out of the South:

> "I hold that a man to gain true self-respect and independence must not be hampered in any way by prejudice. I would remove my school far from such influences."
>
> "Where would your choice fall for the establishment of paradise?" asked Doctor Lewis with a smile.
>
> "There are places enough in the world. *One could easily find such an environment abroad.* There across the water, associated on equal terms with men of the highest culture, the Negro shall give physical utterance to the splendid possibilities which are within him." (389, *emphasis added*)

Curiously, although Hopkins uses the locality to argue that blacks face significant hurdles trying to achieve success in any region of the country, North or South, she does not appear to advocate that African Americans abandon this country altogether. The question of emigration arises during the Canterbury Club dinner, and Mr. Withington asks Will if the government should be held responsible for helping blacks emigrate to another country. Will responds, "Never! . . . Here where we have been so outrageously maligned, let us refute the charges like men!" (300). Will's political stance is to "agitate" for manhood and respectability.

In November 1902, the first installment of *Of One Blood* appeared in the *Colored American Magazine*. Like Will Smith, Reuel Briggs, the main character of this novel, is a young student in search of success. Reuel is also similar to Mark Myers ("The Test of Manhood") in that he leaves the South to test his fortune by passing as a white man in a northern city. Reuel is a promising medical student who knows that he could impress his colleagues with his powers of "mysticism," but his humble background limits his access to the resources he needs: "I have the power, I know the truth of every word—of all M. Binet asserts, and could I but complete the necessary experiments, I would astonish the world. O Poverty, Ostracism! Have I not drained the bitter cup to the dregs!"[22] Reuel remains determined to succeed despite the disadvantages he faces. "Fate had done her worst, but she mockingly beckons me on and I accept her challenge," he states, "I shall not yet attempt the bourne. If I conquer, it will be by strength of brain and will-power. I shall conquer; I must and will" (445). Here Reuel possesses the same ambition and drive of the traditional hero of success novels.

Reuel performs a heroic act when, amid doubt from established doctors, he successfully brings Dianthe Lusk back to life: "Reuel's lucky star was in the ascendant; fame and fortune awaited him; he had but to grasp them. Classmates who had once ignored him now sought familiar association, or else gazed upon him with awe and reverence" (472). Normally, this would be a signal that Reuel is on the road to success, and now that he has achieved some fame, Reuel aims to share his gift with others: "Under pretended indifference to public criticism, throbbed a heart of gold, sensitive to a fault; desiring above all else the well-being of all humanity; his faithfulness to those who suffered amounted to complete self-sacrifice" (473). Still, his racial identity keeps him from finding work when he completes medical school. Despite his professional achievements and noble character, Reuel does not have a support network of friends in high places, as white heroes typically do. After Reuel becomes engaged to Dianthe, he seeks advice from his friend, Aburey Livingston, about how to find gainful employment. Here one would expect Aubrey to help Reuel, but Aubrey proves to be a rival and a false friend who secretly envies Reuel's talents. It is likely that Aubrey spreads rumors about Reuel's racial identity and causes several employment opportunities to be closed to him. Aubrey sends Reuel on an expedition to Africa so that he can have complete access to Dianthe. He conceals his motives from Reuel when he describes the African expedition as one that would bring Reuel fame and success: "It bids fair to be a wonderful venture and there will be plenty of glory for those who return, beside the good it will do to the Negro race if it proves the success in discovery that scholars predict" (494-95). Aubrey is from the South and represents all that is negative about the region: racism, violence, and lust for black women. While Aubrey serves as Reuel's rival, Reuel finds a benefactor in Ai, the prime minister of Telassar, who speaks "in a rich voice, commanding, but with all the benevolence of a father" (545). He is Reuel's true, Afrocentric patron. The narrator writes, "But the most striking thing about the man was his kingly countenance, combining force, sweetness and dignity in every feature" (546). Ai provides him with food, new clothes, a new name, and the ultimate form of gainful employment as ruler of Telassar.

Even though Reuel ends up in Africa because of Aubrey's ulterior motives, this change in environment is significant in that it places Reuel in the right locale to succeed. As Debra Bernardi notes, locations are represented metaphorically and physically in Hopkins's literature. "Her novels can be read as narratives of invasion, narratives that are driven by spatial relocations, as one character invades a new social space, consequently propelling the plot. Social space in Hopkins's work comes to mean physical space used for social purposes . . . as well as the metonymically associated space of the body and, by extension, the psychic space of the mind."[23] Hopkins stresses the impact of racism on a black man's inability to succeed by making the United States a socially hostile space for Reuel, whereas the Ethiopian city of Telassar is a nurturing one. John Gruesser has studied how Hopkins Signifies on white writing about Africa in this novel. "Although she ultimately falls short of providing a radical new way of looking at Africa and the West, Hopkins at times does 'signify on' the conventions of white writing about Africa to produce an Afrocentric fantasy for her black middle-class audience that addresses contemporary race issues."[24] I would add that her use of Africa can also be read as a Signification on the use of space, location, and environment in the traditional success narrative. Instead of finding virtuous heroes in America's heartland, Hopkins places virtue in Africa. Her treatment of Africa and the Afrocentric privileging of Ethiopia is significant. Ethiopia is depicted as the source of high culture and morals, and it becomes a haven for Reuel. For Gruesser, the fact that Hopkins creates this African fantasy for her readers without realistically advocating emigration is a weakness of the novel and her project. He argues that Hopkins is aware that the likelihood that African Americans would reach Africa and recover a glorious ancient heritage is remote.[25] But too much emphasis cannot be placed on the fact that Hopkins is not just contemplating an alternate lifestyle for aspiring blacks, as Gruesser even acknowledges that "*Of One Blood* offers her audience not only a fantasy that restores to Africa its former greatness but also a more local and much needed fantasy, one in which a white American character must answer for racial prejudice and legal segregation."[26] The shift in the setting poignantly removes Reuel from American racial hostility and moves him to a place where he is able to dream and plan for success. Reuel joins the African expedition searching for treasure, and on one visit to the ruins, he dreams "of fame and fortune he would carry home to lay at [Dianthe's] feet" (516). Reuel eventually ends up in the hidden, ancient city of Telassar, and as in traditional success stories, he has moved from the gloomy environment of his dank, third-rate boardinghouse to new, lush surroundings: "He gazed about him in amazement. Gone were all evidences of ruin and decay, and in their place was bewildering beauty that filled him with dazzling awe. He reclined on a couch composed of silken cushions, in a room of vast dimensions, formed of fluted columns of pure white marble upholding a domed ceiling where the light poured in through rose-colored glass in soft prismatic shades which gave a touch of fairyland to the scene" (545).

In another step toward success, Reuel bathes in running water in marble basins with attendants and eats a lavish meal:

> Used as he was to the improvements and luxuries of life in the modern Athens, he could but acknowledge them as poor beside the combination of Oriental and ancient luxury that he now enjoyed. . . . In the air was the perfume and luster of precious incense, the flash of azure and gold, the mingling of deep and delicate hues, the gorgeousness of waving plants in blossom and tall trees—palms, dates, orange, mingled with the gleaming statues that shone forth in brilliant contrast to the dark green foliage. . . .
>
> After the bath came a repast of fruit, game and wine, served him on curious golden dishes that resembled the specimens taken from ruined Pompeii. By the time he had eaten night had fallen, and he laid himself down on the silken cushions of his couch, with a feeling of delicious languor and a desire for repose. (548-49)

In short, at this point, Reuel enjoys a level of material success in Africa that he could not in the United States: "All the dreams of wealth and ambition that had haunted the feverish existence by the winding Charles, that had haunted his days of obscure poverty in the halls of Harvard, were about to be realized" (570). According to Hanna Wallinger, "This movement into the heart of Africa entails for Reuel a movement into his own self, a movement intricately linked to his own racial awakening."[27] I would add that this movement and awakening is a manifestation of his accomplishment of the gospel of success.

At the end of the novel, Reuel leaves the United States to return to Telassar with old Aunt Hannah. Reuel has the support of other people of color, and he in turn serves his people. The whole city of Telassar "lifts him up," and "There he spends his days in teaching his people all that he has learned in years of contact with modern culture. United to Candace, his days glide peacefully by in good works" (621). Reuel cannot successfully apply his education and talents in the United States but he can and does in Africa—for the moment. Hopkins ends the novel with an ambivalent characterization of Africa. If Telassar's civilization is superior to the United States,' why does Reuel need to teach them about Western culture? Even though Hopkins is adamantly against emigration in *Contending Forces*, by 1902 she takes a different position on the subject. In "Famous Women of the Negro Race: Artists" she argues that because it is futile to get whites to respect blacks, blacks should leave the United States:

We have been proving our ability since the days of Phyllis Wheatley and Benjamin Banneker; but it is a hopeless task to undertake to convince a willfully blind and perverse generation. There is but one thing to do for those who have this God-given genius—seek other lands and there accomplish their manhood and womanhood far removed from the blighting influences from which we suffer in this caste-ridden and prejudice-cursed land of our birth. (366)

Still, Hopkins does not explicitly tell her readers to go to Africa. Perhaps Reuel's lessons about "modern" life are a reflection of Hopkins's own disappointment about the need for blacks to follow a path to success that may take them out of the United States to less cultured environs.

Regardless of how one interprets Hopkins's position on African emigration, her stance on the limited opportunities for success in the United States is clear. Hopkins also held particular notions about avenues for success that should be available for African American women, as we shall see in the next chapter.

CHAPTER 4

"In the Lives of These Women are Seen Signs of Progress": Hopkins's Race Woman and the Gospel of Success

In August 1899, a controversy erupted during the second biennial National Association of Colored Women (NACW) convention in Chicago when Josephine St. Pierre Ruffin challenged Mary Church Terrell's election to a second term as NACW president. Ruffin and fellow delegates from the Boston-based Woman's Era Club made allegations of disorganization and ballot tampering. After the convention, once Ruffin's attempt to be elected as the NACW's second president failed, the Woman's Era Club appointed an ad hoc committee to draft resolutions of censure against the association. The Woman's Era Club, which considered itself the authoritative "mother club of the NACW," disapproved of "the conduct of all the business sessions of that convention, [and] the high-handed, unparliamentary rulings of the presiding officer [Terrell], and the unconstitutional elections."[1] Pauline Elizabeth Hopkins, who at this time was an up and coming novelist and journalist, was a member of the Woman's Era Club and served as the ad hoc committee's secretary. Considering the nature of this position, it is safe to assume Hopkins was responsible for drafting the resolutions, which were unanimously adopted by the club, including the recommendation that the Woman's Era Club "withdraw all affiliation with the National Association until such a time as that organization is presided over by constitutionally elected officers."[2] Although the resolutions were approved by the club members, at Ruffin's request they were "laid upon the table for a more careful consideration, and consultation with other clubs in the Federation."[3] The ad hoc committee assented on the condition that their censures be printed in *The National Notes* (the NACW's newsletter) and the *New York Age*, a newspaper edited by T. Thomas Fortune.[4]

Hopkins's participation in what has been called "Mrs. Ruffin's Attacks" illuminates the political interactions that took place between Hopkins and prominent club women.[5] While Hopkins's own activity with the black woman's club movement has already been noted by Hazel Carby, Hanna Wallinger, Lois Brown, and others, little attention has been given to the direct influence club women, namely Josephine St. Pierre Ruffin, have had on Hopkins's literary endeavors. Humanitarian, women's rights advocate, founder of the *Woman's Era*, a national newspaper for African American women, and founder of the Woman's Era Club, Ruffin was a member of Boston's African American upper class and the widow of George Lewis Ruffin, the first African American to graduate from Harvard Law School and one of the first appointed black judges in the nation. Rodger Streitmatter characterizes Ruffin as a resourceful woman who was "financially secure and had a national reputation for her organizational ability and philanthropic endeavors."[6] Mrs. Willis's character in Hopkins's first novel, *Contending Forces*, is a powerful club woman, "the brilliant widow of a bright Negro politician," and just one literary manifestation of Hopkins's interactions with Ruffin (143). Published in 1900, *Contending Forces* was actually completed in 1899, the same year as the contested NACW elections. Mrs. Willis multitasks, overseeing young women in Ma Smith's sewing circle and using a blackboard to review recent events pertinent to the black community. Afterward, Mrs. Willis leads a formal discussion on "The place which the virtuous woman occupies in upbuilding a race" (148). Unfortunately, Mrs. Willis's characterization has been routinely underrated, notwithstanding Siobhan Somerville's assertion that her conversation with Sappho "has an important function in the narrative, as it piques the reader's appetite for the divulgence of Sappho's secret while deferring its exposure."[7] Mrs. Willis is present in only one chapter, and the *Contending Forces* narrator makes ambiguous statements about her motives, but a close reading reveals Hopkins does not share her narrator's sentiments. Albeit a secondary character, Mrs. Willis plays a positive and pivotal role in *Contending Forces*, serving as a black woman's success archetype that, prior to 1900, had been absent from American literature.

A number of literary critics mistakenly assume Hopkins's portrayal of Mrs. Willis is intended to diminish the influence of ambitious black women. Richard Yarborough provides a primary example of this assumption in his introduction to the Oxford edition of *Contending Forces*. Here he argues that Hopkins's feelings toward Mrs. Willis are ambivalent: "Obviously attracted to this woman's strength of mind and forthright feminism, Hopkins seems somewhat unsettled, however, by the extraordinary extent of Willis's driving ambition."[8] By adding an endnote to suggest that Mrs. Willis "may" be modeled after Ruffin, Yarborough implies that Hopkins's conflicted attitude toward this fictive character is indicative of her feelings about the character's historical counterpart.[9] Yarborough's statement, and those of critics who have followed his lead, presume Hopkins's authorial voice and the narrator are one and the same. I, on the other hand, agree with Thomas Cassidy's admonishment that "it is a mistake to identify the narrator of *Contending Forces* with Pauline Hopkins."[10] There is no reason not to connect Mrs. Willis to the real-life Ruffin, and, as Hanna Wallinger notes, "It may be assumed that Hopkins's Boston readers recognized Mrs. Willis as a thinly disguised Mrs. Ruffin and were amused at this."[11] Yet one must keep in mind that Mrs. Willis's actual presence in the novel can be more indicative of Hopkins's attitudes than comments offered by a narrator who Cassidy convincingly argues is "omniscient but unreliable."[12] More important, if one follows the common practice of reading *Contending Forces* squarely within the tradition of domestic and sentimental fiction, then yes, Mrs. Willis's intense ambition and other character traits position her on the margins of the nineteenth-century domestic sphere, leading readers to assume Hopkins intentionally casts her as an unsavory figure. Domestic fiction, however, is just one of the multiple literary genres that Hopkins employs in her work. Situating *Contending Forces*, especially the Sewing-Circle chapter, within the genre of success literature shows Hopkins's tone is less "unsettled" than previously presumed. Indeed, Hopkins adopts and adapts success literature to promote a particular definition of success not only for African American men, but also for African American women, which Josephine St. Pierre Ruffin and Mrs. Willis embody.

Literary scholars routinely situate Hopkins's writings within the sentimental tradition. Yet, sentimental novels did not typically compel readers to seek "explicit expression of their outrage at racial oppression," explains Claudia Tate, but instead "fulfilled the expectations of their first public audience for pleasurable reading in plots affirming the social meaning to which it generally subscribed."[13] In this sense, sentimental novels alone would have been ill-suited for the purposes of a race woman like Hopkins. Domestic fiction, even when it was reconstituted by black women writers, still circumscribed upward-climbing women within a domestic sphere. Politically active black women like Ruffin explicitly opposed being limited to domestic spaces as a means of achieving progress. For example, in the first issue of *Woman's Era*, Ruffin argues, "the stumbling block in the way of even the most cultured colored woman is the narrowness of her environment."[14] Here, as Francesca Sawaya explains, "Ruffin relies on assumptions about progressive civilization much like [white women activists] to criticize the narrowness of both domesticity and 'culture' in a racist society. Black women, she writes, are forced by segregation to exist in a 'circumscribed sphere' the use of the word *sphere* suggesting a kind of enforced domesticity."[15] Other black women, including Hopkins, offer more implicit statements against the suitability of prescribed domestic spheres for all women. I agree with Kate McCullough that "Hopkins used sentimental forms in part because they were among the culturally available and familiar forms of her time; that is, her audience would have known how to read the sentimental signifiers in her work—an important goal given the didactic aim of *Contending Forces*." However, Hopkins also drew upon success literature, which was equally popular during this time period, with its own set of signifiers that readers would have recognized.[16]

Identifying a standard female model of success is challenging because there has not been as much scholarship in this area as there has been on male or gender-neutral success. As Karol Kelley notes in *Models for the Multitudes*, "Female paradigms present certain problems that male paradigms do not. There is no body of literature on feminine success, so female models are harder to find than male models."[17] Nonetheless, she posits that success for women is based on the premise that "In nineteenth-century America there were few occupations open to women which could offer them wealth or status," and as such, motherhood, domesticity, sorority, and true womanhood are factors that have been used to measure a woman's achievements.[18] In essence, the virtues of true womanhood that dominated American society from the 1820s to the 1860s, "piety, purity, submissiveness, and domesticity," continued to create the conditions of success for the late nineteenth- and early twentieth-century woman.[19] According to Barbara Welter, without these virtues, "no matter whether there was fame, achievement or wealth, all was ashes. With them she was promised happiness and power."[20] Interestingly, the expectations of true womanhood did evolve to the point where those who promoted success for women encouraged them to retain their traditional "feminine virtues," along with "a substitution of new elements in the cluster of qualities which comprised the ideal woman. Activity, assertiveness, intelligence, and independence replaced passivity, submission, ignorance, and dependence. . . . She would be seriously devoted to her work, as well as committed to her family. She would work to satisfy her own needs; yet her work would benefit society."[21] In short, the archetypal successful female can be described as a woman who either inherits or marries into money and keeps her feminine virtues intact. Some women did pursue a business enterprise, but because women were still expected to function in separate spheres from men and remain in the domestic space of the home, school, or church, the self-made woman did not exist per se. Most successful women (with a few exceptions) at the turn of the twentieth century achieved influence and wealth through marriage to a successful man.

Although turn of the century African American women are not typically known for their success literature, a number of black women did, in fact, produce conduct literature, success guides, and biographical sketches of accomplished individuals. However, the majority of these works were published after Hopkins's own writings. For example, Hallie Q. Brown's *Homespun Heroines* (1926) contains sixty biographical sketches of black women, including Phillis Wheatley, Sara Allen (wife of A.M.E. church bishop Richard Allen), Josephine St. Pierre Ruffin, and Madam C. J. Walker. These and similar works produced by black women (and men) during this period were typically classified as "race literature," which may have hindered scholars' ability to recognize their contribution to the success genre, particularly in Hopkins's case. One curious specimen written in Hopkins's heyday is Josie Briggs Hall's *Moral and Mental Capsule for the Economic and Domestic Life of the Negro* (1905). In this book, Hall, a native of Texas who taught in multiple schools in the region, offers a range of materials, from biographical sketches of men and women to reprinted essays and poetry, that are designed to instruct black readers "what to do to better their condition" and "to aid the progress of my people."[22] Unlike Hopkins, who was motivated by an intense desire to celebrate the various accomplishments of the race, Hall took the position that blacks were "morally and intellectually weak."[23] Thus the advice that is proffered to those seeking the path to success centers on moral and religion instruction. Hall may have obtained some local recognition for her work—nearly all of the individuals pictured in the book are Texans—but Hopkins developed a national agenda for promoting success within the black community, and she utilized the *Colored American Magazine*'s wide circulation to reach a nationwide audience.

The thematic content of Hopkins's journalism in the *Colored American Magazine* exemplifies how she persisted in applying and modifying the traditional American success myth to the unique social circumstances of the black middle-class community. In "Famous Women of the Negro Race," Hopkins endeavored to construct a separate black woman's paradigm for success by providing her reading audience with historical and contemporary figures worthy of emulation. The *Colored American Magazine*'s "Announcement for 1902" advertises Hopkins's project as "One of the most unique features ever printed by any magazine." Her notions about success echo Ruffin's concerns that "progressive colored women" are not living up to their full potential, "many of them warped and cramped for lack of opportunity."[24] "Can the Negro woman learn anything?" Hopkins asks, and "Is she capable of the highest mental culture? are questions which have been conclusively answered in this series of articles."[25] Defining success archetypes for black women becomes racialized; Hopkins adapts the standard model to defend their intellect and virtue in the first installment: "It is profitable, too, for us to appreciate the fact that the women of the race have always kept pace with every advance made, often leading the upward flight. [. . .] In writing of the attainments of a people it is important that the position of its women be carefully defined—whether endowed with traits of character fit for cultivation, bright intellects and broad humanitarianism, virtuous in all things, tender, loving and of deep religious convictions" ("Phenomenal Vocalists" 46). The cultivation of character and womanhood figure prominently among Hopkins's list of black female attainments. Arguing that black women have been "maligned and misunderstood" but are just as virtuous and gifted as white women, Hopkins offered her series as proof of their equality (46).

Based on the content of her "Famous Women" series, it is apparent that Hopkins measured a black woman's success by the extent to which she utilized her artistic and intellectual talent to uplift the African American community. Hopkins's successful black woman was, ideally, a race woman who married a successful man; simultaneously, the women she spotlighted were particularly adept at their professions. Her subjects were vocalists, writers, educators, artists, and club women who overcame hardship and humble beginnings to use their talents to help benefit and advance the causes of the black community. Hopkins informs readers, for example, that Elizabeth Greenfield had a broad vocal range and could play multiple instruments. She also sang for Queen Victoria while on tour abroad. Annie Pauline Pindell had a broad vocal range and sang in three languages. Phillis Wheatley's "style of writings is pure; her verses full of beauty and sublimity; her language chaste and elegant. Could she have lived a few years longer she would have been renowned as a poet" ("Some Literary Workers" 279). Frances E. W. Harper's intellectual gifts were respected by both whites and blacks: "her ability and labors were everywhere appreciated, and her meetings largely attended. She breakfasted with the Governor of Maine" ("Literary Workers Concluded" 367). Hopkins informs her readers that Mary Church Terrell was so highly respected as a public speaker that she was chosen to represent the white Equal Suffrage Association of Washington at the National Woman's Suffrage Association (370). Fanny Jackson, head of The Institute at Philadelphia, achieved success because "Her ability in governing this institution of learning has given her world-wide fame; she is respected by parents and guardians, and loved by her pupils" ("Educators" 46). Elizabeth Smith, another educator, was noteworthy for using "her wide influence among the young of both races for their elevation and advancement" ("Educators Continued" 126). Thus, achieving renown for one's talents also brought renown to the African American community.

It is not enough that these women were gifted; they used these gifts pragmatically. "If we possess any particular talent," Hopkins writes, "the first question which presents itself to the practical mind is, how this talent can best serve us as a pivot for wage-earning? This is a momentous question for the Negro race at this stage of our progress, when avenues for gathering cold American dollars are gradually lessening for us" ("Artists" 366). Wealth does not receive a lengthy discussion in this series, but Hopkins shows that she is aware of artists' need to earn a living so they can assist others. As an active participant in the black women's club movement, Hopkins devotes the most attention in these articles to black women's racial uplift activities. She contends that through service, both individual women and the African American community can benefit and improve their social, economic, and political status. "In the wonderful scheme of God's earthly government," she argues, "the doing of good to others is the direct means of achieving success in life for ourselves. All science, commerce, industry, spread blessings abroad, leading to fame and fortune if pursued for the benefits spread abroad" ("Higher Education" 446).

It is interesting that Hopkins, who never married, makes a point of showing how successful black women are both intelligent and married. In "Higher Education" she writes, "In reviewing the careers of these young women we must not fail to note one important fact: three of them have become the wives of progressive college men. Education has not caused these women to shirk the cares and responsibilities of private life; rather, we believe each feels the blessing which her example must be to the entire race. Education, with us, does not encourage celibacy but is developing pleasant homes and beautiful families" (450). Most of the women Hopkins included in her series were married. Annie Pindell was married to Joseph Pindell, of a well-known Baltimore family. Gertrude Fortune Grimke, Fanny M. Jackson, Ida B. Wells, and Frances E. W. Harper were married. Hopkins even gave an account of Mary Church and Judge Robert H. Terrell's wedding. One subject, Elizabeth Baker, "is particularly interesting to us by reason of the fame that has come to her husband" (449). Thus Hopkins's agenda in her nonfiction differs slightly from her agenda in her fiction, where she critiques marriageability's central role in the traditional woman's success paradigm. Her journalism provides explicit models for black female readers to aspire to while also illustrating to white readers how intelligent and capable black women are. In her fiction, Hopkins's treatment of female success offers implicit critiques of the traditional archetype that merely judges all women according to the extent to which she has married a successful man. As Mary Helen Washington notes when comparing Hopkins with Frances E. W. Harper, both women "reject the sentimental novel's ideal of marriage as an emotional and economic refuge fore the helpless female; their women heroes marry men for support in their work of racial uplift or they choose uplift over marriage."[26] In *Contending Forces*, for example, black women achieve success both through matrimony with accomplished men (that is, Sappho Clark and Dora Smith's unions with Will Smith and Arthur Lewis, respectively) and also through active participation in the club movement, which Mrs. Willis demonstrates.

A close examination of Mrs. Willis's function in *Contending Forces* reveals how highly Hopkins valued women's ambition beyond the boundaries of childrearing and wedlock, values that are antithetical to the narrator's. We see an early indication of this in a statement the narrator makes about women like Mrs. Willis inhabiting cities throughout the eastern seaboard: "Mrs. Willis was a good example of a class of women of color that came into existence at the close of the Civil War. She was not a *rara avis*, but one of many possibilities which the future will develop from among the colored women of New England" (144). If we take this comment at face value, and trust the narrator's claim that Mrs. Willis is a common type of woman, then we should question why there are no other characters like her in the novel. Hopkins understands Mrs. Willis may well be a rarity to the majority of her readers. She assumes they know little about Mrs. Willis's class and enlightens them accordingly: "Even today it is erroneously believed that all racial development among colored people has taken place since emancipation. It is impossible of belief for some, that little circles of educated men and women of color have existed since the Revolutionary War. [. . .] Mrs. Willis was one from among these classes" (145). Moreover, there are instances when Mrs. Willis's character is cast quite favorably, for example, "At sixty odd she was vigorous, well-preserved, broad and comfortable in appearance, with an aureole of white hair crowning a pleasant face" (145). She is in fine physical shape, the halo-like ring of white hair identifying her as a virtuous matron.

Hopkins uses the two phases of Mrs. Willis's adult life to represent two paths to black women's success. During the first phase, Mrs. Willis is devoted to her husband and his career while remaining at home raising their children: "She had loved her husband with a love ambitious for his advancement. His foot on the stairs mounting to the two-room tenement which constituted their home in the early years of married life, had sent a thrill to her very heart as she sat sewing baby clothes for the always expected addition to the family" (146). She encourages her husband to run for the state legislature, and although a career in politics is not his initial goal, her support helps him become more successful and wealthy. Mrs. Willis's marital life fits the pattern of late nineteenth-century middle-class women assigned to domestic spaces. Even though she is excluded from the business world, she still lives an accomplished life. As Jeffrey Louis Decker explains, "Because women took on the roles of virtuous mothers and supporting wives, entrepreneurial success was mediated through the achievements of men."[27] As a dutiful wife and mother, Mrs. Willis initially experiences financial and social success vicariously through her husband, but when he dies he does not pass on his wealth to her. The narrator does not indicate what has happened to her husband's fortune, only that: "Money, the sinews of living and social standing, she did not possess upon her husband's death" (146). As a result, she enters the second phase of her life and leaves her domestic sphere to earn a living, demonstrating that neither her personal ambitions nor her prospects for success died with her husband. Widowhood, in fact, expands Mrs. Willis's opportunities for advancement. She looks for a means of supporting herself and decides to dedicate herself to "the great cause of the evolution of true womanhood in the work of the 'Woman Question' as embodied in marriage and suffrage" (146). In this way, she matches the profile of women who "became entrepreneurs only after a matrimonial crisis, such as the death or divorce of a husband."[28] There are some similarities between club work and entrepreneurship in terms of the drive and motivation one must have to be successful. Mrs. Willis, in fact, is characterized as a cunning entrepreneur: "Shrewd in business matters, many a subtle business man had been worsted by her apparent womanly weakness and charming simplicity" (144).

Mrs. Willis's character models Hopkins's real-life expectation that "Beyond the common duties peculiar to woman's sphere, the colored woman must have an intimate knowledge of every question that agitates the councils of the world" ("Some Literary Workers" 277). Mrs. Willis represents an archetype of black female success through active participation in the club movement to benefit the race outside the home. "The guiding principle behind all the clubs was racial uplift through self-help," Deborah White notes.[29] In Ma Smith's sewing circle, young African American women use their domestic skills to raise money to improve the church's finances. Discussing political events develops their intellectual abilities and Mrs. Willis's lecture further stresses their moral responsibility to themselves and others. According to Hopkins, a black woman has a particular duty to help the black community because of her "unique position" in society: "Upon the Negro woman lies a great responsibility,—the broadening and deepening of her race, the teaching of youth to grasp present opportunities, and, greater than all, to help clear the moral atmosphere by inculcating a clearer appreciation of the Holy Word and its application to everyday living" ("Some Literary Workers" 277). Active participation in the women's club movement enabled black women to successfully live up to these expectations: "So, through the example of a few public-spirited women, the Negro woman has become ubiquitous in club life, over-flowing into all the avenues of self-help that are adopted by her white sisters as a means to the end of rising herself and 'lifting others as she climbs'" ("Club Life" 274).

Mrs. Willis is a successful advocate for black women. She helps form several colored women's clubs and becomes a powerful leader in her Boston community. Yet, there are some compromises she must make in her line of work, because entrepreneurial women's "marketplace ambitions typically led to the diminishment of their domestic authority as wives and mothers."[30] Mrs. Willis pursues club work only after she has raised her children and supported her husband's political career. She is proud of having had a family: "It was her boast that she had made the fortunes of her family, and settled her children well in life"; yet, once she becomes a public figure, certain aspects of her domestic authority are weakened (147). For example, she inadvertently repels at least one woman she hopes to inspire. Mrs. Willis's comments about the black woman's virtue attract Sappho's attention and compel her to talk with Mrs. Willis about her past: "For a moment the flood-gates of suppressed feeling flew open in the girl's heart, and she longed to lean her head on that motherly breast and unburden her sorrows there" (155). But then, all of a sudden, Sappho changes her mind and becomes reticent as "a wave of repulsion toward this woman and her effusiveness, so forced and insincere" keeps her from divulging her secret (155).

Yarborough calls attention to this scene to support his theory that Sappho's repulsion mirrors Hopkins's true position on Mrs. Willis's conduct. Other literary critics have followed Yarborough's lead. Siobhan Somerville argues that Mrs. Willis's portrayal "symbolized ambivalence about the possibility of women's solidarity."[31] Thomas Cassidy suggests, "Sappho's ambivalence toward her seems to reflect the narrator's. The problem with Mrs. Willis is that she is too slick."[32] Hanna Wallinger observes that Hopkins's portrayal of Mrs. Willis is "not totally positive. The heroine Sappho especially resents Mrs. Willis's attempt to meddle in her affairs, her effusive and inquisitive manner and her officiousness."[33] Apparently seizing on the narrator's comment that Mrs. Willis's designs for concentrating her efforts on the Woman Question are "conceived in selfishness" (147), Claudia Tate goes as far as to argue that Mrs. Willis is a "successful but problematic professional woman": "She revises the traditional role of the retiring, reticent, widowed matron to become an outspoken race woman who attracts ambivalence precisely because she seeks self-authority rather than selflessness."[34] Selfless acts may be requisite of the sentimental matron, but not of the successful woman. What is more important to Hopkins is not how one's plans are conceived but their outcome, which in Mrs. Willis's case "bore glorious fruit in the formation of clubs of colored women banded together for charity, for study, for every reason under God's glorious heavens that can better the condition of mankind" (147). Josephine St. Pierre Ruffin utilized this success rhetoric during an 1895 convention address when she identified issues "of especial interest to us as *colored* women," including not only children's education, vocational training for black youth, and moral education for the black community, but also black women's own "mental elevation and physical development" and the means "to make the most of our own, to some extent limited opportunities."[35] Ruffin established a precedent for Mrs. Willis, who employs the same success rhetoric to encourage Sappho to "stand up for uplifting of the race and womanhood" (156).

Mrs. Willis's "sheer force of will-power and indomitable pluck" (148) does challenge Hopkins to depict her as a believable and sympathetic character. Tate recognizes Mrs. Willis's unconventionality and argues Hopkins "could not resolve the discomfort of her contemporaries about female will to power," but "she could mitigate its effect by deploying what Fredric Jameson has called 'strategies of containment,' which is to say that she allows Sappho to voice and control the likely expression of her contemporaries' objections."[36] I think Hopkins ultimately mitigates this discomfort by drawing on the literary tradition of success instead of sentimentalism. When Sappho obsesses over how her past transgressions, committed under duress, will affect her marriageability, Mrs. Willis proclaims, "See here, my dear, I am a practical woman of the world" (156). Mrs. Willis draws from her sagacious understanding of human nature to assure Sappho that she need only "have faith and trust" in order to fulfill her duty to herself "and the good of those about [her]" (157). Our last image of Mrs. Willis is of her vanishing "in a crowd of other matrons" (157). Sappho is "impressed in spite of herself, by the woman's words," which leads the narrator to conclude: "There was evidently more in this woman than appeared upon the surface. [. . .] There are men and women whose seeming uselessness fit perfectly into the warp and woof of Destiny's web. All things work together for good" (157). Even though the narrator initially suggests that Mrs. Willis's mien renders her an ineffective mentor, in this final comment, the narrator unwittingly gives credence to Mrs. Willis's driving ambition, beneficent work, and sage advice. Hopkins's faith in the positive role Mrs. Willis's pragmatism plays in black women's as well as broader racial uplift movements is certainly more constant than the narrator's.

Hopkins broke new ground with Mrs. Willis's character. With the exception of Frances E. W. Harper's racially ambiguous Janette Alston in "The Two Offers" (1859), black women did not depict such forcefully independent and successful female characters in their fiction. Mrs. Willis's character serves as one of Hopkins's first attempts to move beyond the parameters of sentimental literature to offer alternative models of success for black women. Hopkins is like other advocates who "dangled a dramatic vision of a successful woman before their audience and invited members of their audience to become that ideal."[37] By the conclusion of *Contending Forces*, Sappho has married "the noblest of men" and has succeeded in creating a family with Will and Alphonse (401). The "life of promise" she happily contemplates is not complete with matrimony and motherhood, however. Sappho, like Mrs. Willis before her, is destined to achieve eminence and respectability through matrimony *and* racial uplift: "United by love, chastened by sorrow and self-sacrifice, [Will and Sappho] planned to work together to bring joy to hearts crushed by despair" (401).

The other women in *Contending Forces* experience varying degrees of success, which is often dependent on their marital status or husbands' accomplishments. For example, Grace Montfort is married to a white Bermudan slave owner and fits the traditional model of the successful woman who marries into wealth. Charles Montfort's success enables Grace to live happily, and when he decides to relocate his estate to the United States, we witness how closely her fate is tied to his business decisions. Grace is initially well-received in Newbern, North Carolina, society and noted for her high culture, virtue, and beauty: "Everyone voted her the dearest and most beautiful woman they had ever known, and all would have gone merry as a marriage-bell," but for Anson Pollock (45). When Pollock declares his love to Grace, she responds as a faithful wife, rejecting Pollock's advances: "Am I so careless of my husband's honor that his friends feel at liberty to insult me?" (50). Grace begins to lose her social standing after rumors are spread about her having black blood. Montfort's plan to free his slaves also ostracizes her from her community. It is not clear if Pollock actually believes Grace is a descendant of African Americans, but he does use the rumors to destroy her marriage and her home. Pollock takes advantage of the white Newbern community's racist attitude toward people of mixed racial heritage to make the Montforts vulnerable to racially motivated violence. Hopkins neither confirms nor denies Grace's black ancestry in order to argue that the mere implication of such ancestry is damaging enough to Grace's ability to live a successful life. Hazel Carby's assessment of Grace's racial ambiguity is cogent: "Hopkins made it clear that it was irrelevant whether Grace Montfort was a black or a white woman. . . . The readers were left to guess her actual heritage; what was important was that the suspicion of black blood was enough cause for the ostracism of the whole family and Grace Montfort's transition from the pedestal of virtue to the illicit object of the sexual desire of a local landowner, Anson Pollock."[38] Once Grace becomes black in the white community's eyes, her husband can no longer protect her. Without this protection, Grace cannot be a successful wife or mother. Tragedy strikes when Pollock's gang murders her husband, rapes her, and remands her and her children to slavery. She commits suicide instead of resigning to live the life of a slave. Hopkins clearly depicts Grace as a victim, but Grace ends her life as a failure. Hopkins reverses the trajectory of the self-made woman, allowing Grace to fall from prominence to despair, in order to critique the sensibility of a culture that encourages, if not demands, women to rely entirely on their husbands for success.

Dora Smith, another black woman depicted in the novel whose fate is tied to her husband's pursuit of success, is initially in charge of the day-to-day operations of her mother's boardinghouse. By the end of the novel she has married Arthur Lewis, a prestigious college president. Once Dora gets married, she does not need to earn an income for her family. Interestingly, Hopkins depicts Dora as happily married, a "contented young matron, her own individuality swallowed up in love for her husband and child" (389–90). It would not be difficult to read Dora's marital life as a sacrifice of a woman's individuality for the black family. On the one hand, Dora dispels stereotypes of the oversexed, immoral black woman. Still, her married life appears limited, especially when compared with Sappho Clark's.

Like Grace Montfort, Sappho comes close to failing in life because of the stigma of her racial heritage. She is a self-employed stenographer with a mysterious past who works in her room at Ma Smith's boardinghouse. Although she cannot work in her employer's office because he does not want to offend his white workers, his brand of racism does not prevent her from earning a living. Interestingly, even though Sappho is self-employed and independent, she still dreams of having a legitimate marriage. This would lead one to believe that Hopkins privileges married women over single working women, but this is not necessarily the case. Readers learn that she is really Mabelle Beaubean, a young woman who had been kidnapped by her white uncle and forced into prostitution. Sappho had a child at the age of fourteen and is haunted by her past life. Because she has had a child out of wedlock, Sappho fears she is unworthy of an honorable man's love and hand in marriage. She tells Mrs. Willis, "So many of us desire purity and think to have found it, but in a moment of passion, or under the pressure of circumstances which we cannot control, we commit some horrid sin, and the taint of it sticks and will not leave us, and we grow to loathe ourselves" (154). Furthermore, when Will proposes to Sappho, she questions her right to happiness and thus to success: "Ah, Will, I wonder if it is right for me to love you, or to allow you to love me?" (311). Sappho does not have family, friends, or money, but this does not deter Will, who does not care to know about her past even though she tries to tell him about it. Despite her shameful secret,

Sappho falls in love and plans to marry Will. Because Will is a promising student who, unbeknownst to anyone, stands to inherit a small fortune, Hopkins places Sappho in a position to become a successful woman.

John Langley, Will's false friend, stands as an obstacle in Sappho's path to success. When he suspects that he knows Sappho's secret, he confronts her and offers to "do well" by her if she is willing to give up Will. Sappho mistakes his offer for a marriage proposal, but Langley has other plans: "Marriage! . . . who spoke of marriage? Ambitious men do not marry women with stories like yours!" (320). All hope seems lost for Sappho as she considers "the abyss of social ostracism and disgrace which confronted her" (320), and she decides to flee Boston. Like Grace Montfort, Sappho is forced to run from a man who is determined to use her racial identity to victimize her and strip her of her womanhood. John Langley attempts to blackmail her into becoming his mistress. Dora's comment on Sappho's condition, and that of women in a similar situation, is apt: "Oh, that poor, miserable girl! think [sic] of her sufferings—of the weight of the secret she carried with her. What a crucifixion for a proud spirit like hers! This terrible curse of slavery! Shall we never lose the sting of degradation?" (330). Because of the African American woman's sexual victimization during slavery, she developed a reputation for loose morals, and both white and black men assumed she was easy prey. Indeed, Sappho's life had been "made dark and desolate by the curse of slavery" (343). Yet, Sappho steps back on the path to success by claiming her son, Alphonse. She resolves to "do her duty as his mother in love and training" (342). As she gazes at her sleeping son, Sappho realizes that she "had been so wicked to put him from her. It was her duty to guide and care for him. She would do her duty without shrinking" (345). Hopkins devotes some time to detailing Sappho's feelings about motherhood, and thus reiterates the point that black women should be dedicated to their own success as well as others.

Hopkins's treatment of black women's success in *Contending Forces* concentrates on critiquing the assumptions whites (and some blacks) held about a black woman's ability to sustain a successful marital relationship in the age of Jim Crow. Hopkins's second novel, *Hagar's Daughter*, also depicts multiple models of marriage that can be used to measure black women's success. Hopkins establishes the tone of critique early in the novel, depicting various black marriages being broken up at a slave auction. She calls the reader's attention to a group of female slaves, including one who "had been separated from her husband, and another woman whose looks expressed the anguish of her heart."[39] A slave trader approaches another weeping woman and offers to give her a new spouse. "I don't want anudder mon," she responds, "an' I tell you, massa, I nebber will hab anudder mon" (10). These women are heartbroken and distraught over losing their mates, and here Hopkins attempts to dispel the myth that the institution of marriage has no lasting value in the black community. She also raises readers' awareness of how vulnerable black women are when they can be separated from their husbands so easily.

Like Grace Montfort, Hagar Sargeant marries a wealthy slave holder; Ellis Enson is "a well-made man. . . . 'Born with a silver spoon in his mouth'" (31). Hagar's marriage to Ellis facilitates her blossoming into womanhood: "She had matured wonderfully in the few months of married life; her girlish manner had dropped from her like a garment. Eve's perfect daughter, she accomplished her destiny in sweet content" (46). This description of Hagar's idyllic marriage establishes a contrast for its eventual destruction. Suspicion of Hagar's racial heritage, coupled with St. Clair Enson's jealousy, leads to the demise of her marriage. After St. Clair and a slave trader named Walker present Ellis with documentation that Hagar has black blood, Hagar feels the impact of her invalid marriage almost immediately: "Her name gone, her pride of birth shattered in one blow! . . . Her education, beauty, refinement, what did they profit her now if—horrible thought—Ellis, her husband, repudiated her?" (57). Hagar realizes she can be nothing more than Ellis's concubine, and he initially rejects her to protect his honor and family name. Shortly thereafter he realizes he cannot leave his wife and daughter, and he makes plans for them to leave their plantation and live abroad in Europe. Meanwhile, as news of Hagar's ethnicity spreads, she is deemed a failure: "Here was a woman raised as one of a superior race, refined, cultured, possessed of all the Christian virtues, who would have remained in this social sphere all her life, beloved and respected by her descendants, her blood mingling with the best blood of the country if untoward circumstances had not exposed her ancestry. But the one drop of black blood neutralized all her virtues, and she became, from the moment of exposure, an unclean thing" (62). Unfortunately, Hagar's and Ellis's plans are interrupted for a time when St. Clair attacks his brother and sells Hagar into slavery. She, like Grace Montfort, tries to drown herself rather than remain a slave. Readers presume she commits suicide until the conclusion of the story reveals that she and her daughter survived.

Hagar finds some degree of success married to the wealthy Senator Bowen. As the senator's second wife, "Mrs. Bowen simply fulfilled woman's mission in making her husband's career successful by the exercise of her own intuitive powers" (82). Being his wife has its rewards, and as Hagar tends to her dying husband, the narrator comments: "Wealth she might have, but it would not supply the tender deference and loving solicitude of wedded life that had been hers" (196). Indeed, Bowen bestows Hagar with her reward and "confirmation" of her success when he awakens from his coma and tells her,

"You have been a perfect wife. I have left you well provided for" (197). Yet, race prejudice continues to threaten her happiness after her own daughter's efforts to maintain a successful marriage fail.

Like a number of heroines in female success stories, Jewel Bowen, Hagar's daughter, comes from a privileged family. Twice Jewel is in the position to inherit a wealthy estate, first as Ellis Enson's biological daughter and then as Senator Bowen's adopted daughter. During the course of the novel, Jewel is engaged and later married to Cuthbert Sumner, who also comes from a prominent family. Their relationship is put to the test when Aurelia Madison and General Benson (a.k.a. St. Clair Enson) plot to break up their union. Although they remain faithful to each other, their marriage and Jewel's success are jeopardized when Jewel's racial heritage is discovered. Although initially prejudiced against African Americans, Cuthbert decides to remain married to his beloved Jewel. Unfortunately, it takes Cuthbert some time to overcome his prejudices, and by the time he finds the Ensons, Jewel has died of Roman fever while in Europe.

Hopkins's treatment of Aurelia Madison's character is among the most dynamic because she depicts her as an *anti*-Alger heroine while subverting the conventions of the young woman's success novel. Almost all of Horatio Alger's success novels have male heroes, with a few rare exceptions like *Helen Ford*. Although Alger published this novel in 1866, two years before his most well-known novel, *Ragged Dick*, the plot is very similar to his later rags-to-riches tales. The gender-specific conventions of women's success fiction, which Hopkins adapts in *Hagar's Daughter*, include the heroine's employment outside the traditional women's domestic sphere, and marriage, which removes her from the streets, places her back in the home and allows her to thrive there as a wife and mother. Like Helen Ford, Aurelia Madison's mother is dead and her father raises her. Helen and her father have a close relationship wherein Helen assumes the maternal functions of their transient household. Her father is too distracted with his flying machine invention to serve as a competent father figure for Helen. Major Madison is similarly preoccupied with his own enterprises, but unlike Helen Ford, Aurelia suffers from his lack of guidance. Aurelia spends her early childhood in a convent, and once she leaves, she spends a substantial amount of time in her father's gambling parlor. Hopkins implies that the Major uses Aurelia to lure unsuspecting men into the house so that he can cheat them out of their money. "Washington society," she writes, "with its proneness to overlook small trespasses, was beginning to talk about the Madisons. Some declared the beautiful daughter but a bait to snare the unwary, and openly voted the Major 'shady'" (130). Even though Aurelia is an independent woman, she ventures in spheres that are inappropriate for true women. She is always the only woman present in her father's drawing room, for example. Aurelia's presence in the gambling parlor illustrates how she is working outside the traditional domestic sphere. Helen Ford accepts a job as an actress to support herself and her father. Even though she willingly puts herself on public display each night, she does so while remaining virtuous and modest. For example, she maintains an appropriate level of embarrassment about having to walk home from the theater at night without an escort. Aurelia, on the other hand, is always flamboyant when she appears in public. She is beautiful, but also sensuous to a fault. Hopkins's description of the dress Aurelia wears to the Bowens' ball is a typical example of the manner in which she frequently characterizes Aurelia's warm, scarlet sensuality: "This woman was quite the loveliest thing they had ever seen, startling and somewhat bizarre, perhaps, but still marvelously, undeniably lovely. Her gown was a splendid creation of scarlet and gold. It was a magnificent and daring combination . . . but it bewildered one so that the eye rested on Jewel's slender, white-robed figure with pleasure, and intense relief" (115–16). Aurelia is accustomed to using her body and physical beauty to get what she wants. We should remember, however, that Aurelia's white father and his white associate encourage her to behave in this manner.

At one point Aurelia is engaged to Cuthbert Sumner, but he breaks off the engagement after discovering that she flirts with other men. Because Aurelia is not an ideal wife, her prospects for success are grim. Cuthbert thinks, "she was not the woman to command the respect of his friends nor to bring him complete happiness" (92). What seals Aurelia's fate is the revelation that she is the daughter of Major Madison's slave-mistress and that she has black blood. Traditionally, the discovery of the heroine's true identity facilitates her eventual success. In *Helen Ford,* Helen and her father turn out to be lost heirs to a fortune. In *Hagar's Daughter,* Aurelia's black blood ensures that she inherits a lifetime of misery. When Cuthbert confronts her about her race, she is defiant: "If the world is to condemn me as the descendant of a race that I abhor," she says, "it shall never condemn me as a coward!" (238). At the conclusion of the novel, it is clear that Aurelia fails to achieve success: " . . . the close of the trail would see her homeless, friendless, moneyless, under the ban of a terrible caste prejudice . . ." (242). But, in the end, no criminal charges are brought against Aurelia for her misdeeds, "in fact, no one desired to inflict more punishment on the unfortunate woman" (272). By the novel's end she has vanished into seclusion. Ultimately, the dynamics of race prejudice prevent Aurelia from marrying and becoming a successful woman. Aurelia is a woman of African American descent who bitterly hates her ethnic identity because she knows it places her in a vulnerable position in society. The men in her life assume her virtue needs no protection.

Cuthbert abandons her, and her father sacrifices her true womanhood for the benefit of his own bank account. Yet, despite Aurelia's treacherous behavior, Hopkins chooses not to condemn her. Instead, Hopkins condemns the residual effects slavery has had on black womanhood and black women's ability to succeed in the United States. Elise Bradford, a minor character, explains why we should not hate women like Aurelia but pity them instead: "Socially, they are not recognized by the whites; they are often without money enough to bu[y] the barest necessities of life; honorably, they cannot procure sufficient means to gratify their luxurious tastes. . . . [D]ebauched whitemen [sic] are ever ready to take advantage of their destitution, and after living a short life of shame, they sink into early graves. . . . You know yourself Mr. Sumner, that caste as found at the North is a terrible thing. It is killing the black man's hope there in every avenue; it is centered against his advancement" (159). Hopkins's tone toward Aurelia is sympathetic, for she is "but another type of the products of the accursed system of slavery. . . . There was something, too, that compelled admiration in this resolute standing to her guns with the determination to face the worst that fate might have in store for her" (238).

Another biracial character who develops "resolute standing" is Winona, the heroine of Hopkins's third novel. Elizabeth Ammons observes that Hopkins employs multiple literary traditions in *Winona:* "Generically the novel combines the western, fugitive slave narrative, romance, pot boiler/ soap opera, political novel, and traditional allegory to tell the story of the paradisiacal possibility but real life destruction of a truly mixed-race North American family."[40] On the surface this novel may not appear to map to the typical success novel; however, if we consider the manner in which this novel of development follows conventions of the bildungsroman, a close relative of the success novel, then we can observe how Hopkins continues her project of Signifying on traditional literary forms to create success literature germane to the African American experience. The term *bildungsroman* was originally used to designate a particular novel form that focused on the psychological development of its protagonist, and it flourished in Germany in the eighteenth and nineteenth centuries. Goethe's *Wilhelm Meister's Lehrjahre* (1794–96) is considered the prototype. According to Jerome Buckley, the bildungsroman has also been known as "the novel of youth, the novel of education, of apprenticeship, of adolescence, of initiation, even the life-novel."[41] Though the term escapes "precise definition or neat translation," today it is generally used to designate a novel that traces a protagonist's development from childhood through adolescence and into early adulthood, as he or she negotiates questions about his or her place in society.[42] Scholars who have identified the bildungsroman in African American literature observe how this genre "in the hands of ethnic authors, often [thematizes] ethnicity."[43] In *Winona*, the heroine, a fair-skinned and beautiful quadroon, is orphaned when her self-exiled British father, White Eagle, is mysteriously murdered. She is remanded to slavery but eventually freed by Warren Maxwell, a British attorney, and Ebenezer Maybee, a white hotel proprietor who is sympathetic to the abolitionist movement. During the course of the novel, the implications of Winona's ethnic identity disrupt her peaceful and tranquil adolescence, as she learns what it means to be a biracial woman in the United States. As Winona matures and develops romantic feelings for Maxwell, Hopkins returns to her argument that the conditions for black American women's success are unstable in the United States. Not only does Hopkins adopt and adapt the bildungsroman, but she also invokes the rhetoric of the Manifest Destiny ideology to present a sophisticated critique of the gospel of success, especially the belief that unfettered dreams can become realities in the United States of America. At first glance *Winona* seems to focus more on Maxwell's development than the heroine's, despite the title's connotation. Like William Wells Brown's heroine Clotel, Winona does not develop a memorable presence nor a strong voice until the plot is well underway. As "an incredibly virtuous but almost invisible heroine," to use Ammon's phrasing, readers are inclined to dismiss Winona and focus their attention on characters that appear to be more dynamic, like Judah and Maxwell.[44] Yet we underestimate the extent of Hopkins's social critique if we interpret Winona's character as simply another tragic mulatta typically found in sentimental fiction of the period. If we read this novel as a modified bildungsroman, as a young black woman's narrative of psychological development, then we witness once again Hopkins advocating a success paradigm that is not individualistic but communal and that hinges upon one's ability to escape race-based social and political policies.

According to Buckley, in the bildungsroman, "A child of some sensibility grows up in the country, or in a provincial town, where he finds constraints, social and intellectual, placed upon the free imagination. His family, especially his father, proves doggedly hostile to his creative instincts or flights of fancy, [and] antagonistic to his ambitions."[45] As the novel opens, Winona is depicted as a free-spirited and fanciful young teenager who relishes her natural surroundings on Lake Erie. White Eagle's remote island homestead contains "deer-paths winding through the woods, the green world still in its primal existence in this forgotten spot brought back the golden period unknown to the world living now in anxiety and toil."[46] Winona spends her days picking flowers, observing squirrels and black birds, and reflecting on Old Nokomis's tales of Native American folklore. An exchange between Winona and her adopted brother, Judah, reveals the potential White Eagle has to disrupt Winona's "flights of fancy." When Judah reminds Winona that she will be entering a convent and receiving a formal education from nuns, Winona declares that she will not comply with her father's wishes: "Papa cannot make me. I will not" (293). Winona resists the limitations that she instinctively knows will be placed upon her "free imagination." White Eagle is murdered before he has the opportunity to assert his paternal authority on Winona, but because White Eagle's murderer and Winona's kidnapper, White Eagle's cousin Colonel Titus, hails from her paternal family line, Winona's freedom is still usurped in accordance with the bildungsroman tradition.

Buckley explains that in the typical bildungsroman, the protagonist's "first schooling, even if not totally inadequate, may be frustrating insofar as it may suggest options not available to him in his present settings. He therefore, sometimes at a quite early age, leaves the repressive atmosphere of home (and also the relative innocence), to make his way independently in the city."[47] The "first schooling" Winona receives is in indigenous folklore. Old Nokomis instructs Winona in botanicals and "spirits" (292). Hopkins breaks from the bildungsroman tradition when Winona is kidnapped from home instead of being forced to enter the "repressive atmosphere" of a convent inhabited by "a lot of nuns and strange girls who do not care for [her]" (293). A Missouri plantation functions as the ultimate repressive atmosphere. While Winona receives a conventional education on Colonel Titus's plantation along with her young mistress, the Colonel believes Winona's music and reading lessons will increase her market value and "pay ten dollars for every one invested" because he considers her merely chattel (320). Winona also learns of the realities of racial prejudice as the assault upon her innocence commences. Here, "In the life she had led as a slave, this poor child had learned things from which the doting mother guards the tender maidenhood of her treasure with rigid care; so the girl thought of marriage or its form, with the utmost freedom" (356). On this plantation Titus functions as a surrogate paternal figure who impedes Winona's emerging ambitions by enslaving her and subordinating her well-being for his own greed.

According to Martin Japtok, the traditional bildungsroman form "predominantly stress[es] the individual but may also acknowledge a community; ethnic texts feature community involvement more predominantly, but they also stress individual development, so that communalism and individualism exist side by side."[48] Hopkins creates a nurturing foster community in John Brown's camp. Once Winona is rescued from Titus's plantation, this veritable village embraces the orphan. Here, Winona and other fugitive slaves receive their "first lessons in the true principles of home-building and the responsibility of freedom" (374). Prior to Winona's abduction, she had been reared among a "mixed community of Anglo-Saxons, Indians and Negroes" (287). In the camp, which is similarly diverse, "the great family of fugitives dwelt together in guileless and trusting brotherhood under the patriarchal care of Captain Brown" (373). Just as *Contending Forces* and the "Famous Women" series privilege communal relationships and uplift activities, *Winona* stresses that a successful outcome of Winona's psychological developmental journey is dependent upon the good intentions and actions of others. Winona is not an entirely passive figure, however. Maxwell's capture presents the opportunity for her to enter and complete the apprentice stage of her development. When she learns that Maxwell is being held captive, she seeks solitude and creeps "into the woods not to weep, but to think" (380). Winona prays for the wherewithal to save Maxwell. As Buckley notes, once the typical bildungsroman hero "has decided, after painful soul-searching, the sort of accommodation to the modern world he can honestly make, he has left his adolescence behind and entered upon his maturity."[49] Similarly, Winona searches within herself and "In the morning she sought an interview with Captain Brown" (380). With Brown's approval, Winona disguises herself as a young boy, Allen Pinks, and returns to Missouri to nurse Maxwell and facilitate his escape from jail. Winona demonstrates her maturity and competence when Maxwell is successfully rescued. Later she is left "in command of the home guard" (409), having proven her competence to lead and having completed the apprentice stage of her development.

Like Buckley's bildungsroman hero, Winona's story includes an "ordeal by love."[50] She becomes self-conscious after rescuing Maxwell, and "little by little, a gulf had opened between them which to her unsophisticated mind could not be bridged" (404). One source of this gulf is her assumption that she "was nothing" to Maxwell because of her race (405). In typical bildungsroman fashion, Winona experiences painful soul searching as she tries to determine what her place in American society is as long as slavery and racial prejudice persist. "Which is my country, I wonder?" she asks, " . . . This country mine? No, no! The fearful things that I have seen. . . . My father's country shall be mine" (406). While Maxwell encourages her to consider the possibilities of marriage, Winona resolves to enter a convent. It is not until her true identity as Henry Carlingford's daughter is confirmed that Winona is free to marry Maxwell. Once in England, Winona is "a noble woman"; "all worshipped the last beautiful representative of ancient family" (435).

Interestingly, to show how the myth of success crosses racial and even national boundaries, Hopkins includes another narrative of development in this novel that parallels Winona's. Warren Maxell's character is also employed to critique the gospel of success in the United States. Through Maxwell, readers learn how inalienable human rights are jeopardized by institutionalized slavery. The phrase Manifest Destiny was coined by John L. O'Sullivan and first used in the 1840s to justify United States expansion into Texas, Oregon, and Mexico. Broadly speaking, the ideology subscribes to the belief that the United States was destined by Providence to expand its borders and territories to the far West of the North American continent. The doctrine of Manifest Destiny also included fear of British expansion into North America. As the United States acquired additional territories, and as these territories applied for statehood, the nation was forced to consider the extent to which slavery would also be expanded across the United States. Hopkins uses the rhetoric of Manifest Destiny to illustrate how American racism was unique and made conditions for success nearly impossible within its borders. Hopkins revisits the argument she makes in *Peculiar Sam* and *Contending Forces* (and would make again in *Of One Blood*) about the United States being unfit to foster African American success. *Winona* presents a more sophisticated rendering of United States national policy and its impact on African American success and progress.

Hopkins introduces the doctrine of Manifest Destiny and establishes the foundation for her critique when she describes the history of the novel's setting. The opening setting is on the border, no-man's land on an island within Lake Erie, between Canada and New York state: "From 1842, the aborigines began to scatter. They gave up the last of this great reservations then before the on-sweeping Anglo-Saxon, moving toward the setting sun in the pasture lands surrounding the Black Hills" (287). We also learn that "Yet, through Erie County urged the Indians farther West, and took up their reservations for white settlers, their thirst for power stopped short of the curtailment of human liberty. The free air of the land of the prairies was not polluted by the foul breath of slavery" (288).

Warren Maxwell accepts an assignment from his British law firm to find the lost heir to the Carlingford estate, for doing so will give him the opportunity to establish a respectable reputation and acquire affluence: "But he had come with a purpose; he was determined to succeed. There were three others at home older than himself; his own share in the family estate would amount to an annuity scarcely enough to defray his tailor's bill. . . . In family council, therefore, it was decided that law, with money and old family influence might lead to Parliament in the future; and so Warren took up the work determined to do his best" (298). If Maxwell completes his mission to America successfully, his employers "would be generous—in fact, he would become a full partner, sharing all the emoluments of the position at once" (299).

When Maxwell first meets Judah and Winona he is naïve and does not quite understand how their status as "only niggers and Injuns" could affect their lives: "Still they're human beings, and entitled to some consideration," he says (303). As Maxwell comes to understand the American caste system, he pities Winona and pledges to help her, knowing that "In England, neither their color nor race will be against them. They will be happier there than here" (311). As Maxwell becomes more involved in Winona's and Judah's lives, he receives an education of his own. He expects his rights to be respected and honored because he is a British subject, but they are not. Maxwell vows to "appeal to the British consul for protection from your vile insults" (380–81): "He meditated upon his position in the heart of a hostile country although supposed to advocate and champion the most advanced ideas of liberty and human rights. What a travesty the American government was on the noblest principles!" (381). He draws up a protest, which he declares in open court, but it is thrown aside by the magistrate. Maxwell's education is not complete until he is freed and joins John Brown and Maybee. "I understand the slavery question through and through," he says. "Experience is a stern teacher" (395).

By recasting the marriage plot, Hopkins argues that racism in the United States prevents black women from realizing their dream of having a stable family, and thus racism prevents black women from experiencing success. At the conclusion of *Hagar's Daughter*, Hopkins offers a final comment about the impact slavery and racism have on a black woman's inability to achieve success through marriage: "The holy institution of marriage ignored the life of the slave, breed [sic] indifference in the masters to the enormity of illicit connections, with the result that the sacred family relation is weakened and finally ignored in many cases" (284). For Hopkins, all black women are victims of slavery and its residual racism. Hopkins's use of fiction Signifies on popular tropes of success literature to demonstrate how racism inhibits true African American women's success. One question remains: Would Hopkins, who did not marry but rather followed Mrs. Willis's alternative path to success by concentrating her energies on her writing career and club activities, have considered herself a success? Her work on behalf of racial uplift, black women's clubs, and the *Colored American Magazine* qualify as successful achievements by her own standards.

Conclusion

"Let the Good Work Go On"

A number of other questions remain about Hopkins's project, like how effective were her articles at motivating young blacks to seek moderate wealth and respectability through self-help and uplift? If given the opportunity, did they choose to model their lives after her success archetypes in the "Famous Men of the Negro Race" and "Famous Women of the Negro Race" series, or did they prefer to follow the examples set by Booker T. Washington? Furthermore, did Hopkins's criticism of the racism and sexism inherent in the traditional gospel of success enlighten any of her white readers? To answer these questions, we would need to know more about the reception history of Hopkins's work. Unfortunately, the amount of documentary evidence available that would provide enough insight into the effectiveness of her project is scant. Judging from the magazine's circulation totals during Hopkins's tenure and afterward, it appears that readers did prefer the journal's literary content instead of the business content, and they may have found some value in her short stories and novels that depicted the black success archetype. In Hopkins's letter to Trotter, written less than one year after she left the *Colored American Magazine*, she claimed, "The agents in every city have complained bitterly of the change of policy; it has hurt their sales; many of them have given the book up. In New York City we sold from 800 to 1500 per month; under the new policy the sales have shrunk to 200 per month and the magazine would be out of business were it not for the fact that it is supported from Mr. Washington's private purse. Nor did the whites rally to the support of the pitiful rag issued each month which was but a shadow of its former self."[1] The magazine finally ceased publication in 1909, shortly after Washington withdrew his interest and financial support. A number of letters sent to the editor of the *Colored American Magazine* during Hopkins's tenure there offer general support for the magazine, but it does not appear that any readers responded directly to Hopkins's prescription for black success. For example,

T. Thomas Fortune, the black editor of the *New York Age*, and Daniel Murray, a black employee of the Library of Congress, both responded favorably to the magazine's appearance and credibility.[2] Alberta Moore Smith, an active black club woman, gave *Contending Forces* a favorable review, but she did not take note of Hopkins's treatment of African American success in the novel: "It is undoubtedly the book of the century. . . . This book should be classed as one of the standard works of the day."[3] Thus, it seems that most of the black response to Hopkins's work was favorable, albeit in a general sense as race literature, not necessarily as success literature.

The pages of the *Colored American Magazine* do reveal the interesting advertising history for *Contending Forces*, the novel that probably contains Hopkins's most comprehensive treatment of African American success. The book was advertised frequently in the *Colored American Magazine* from 1900 to 1902. A September 1900 advertisement, one of the first, offered the novel for sale by subscription for $1.50. In October 1900, the editorial board proudly announced that advance sales of the book "have been enormous."[4] But in July 1901, the management decided to change its marketing tactics and offered the novel to readers free for the asking, with no strings attached: "It is our desire to distribute a FREE COPY of it in every section of the country as we feel sure that where it is once introduced, we will sell hundreds of copies."[5] *Contending Forces* continued to be offered for free or at a discount until the spring of 1902. Specific sales figures are needed to determine if the free book offer was successful. Still, considering the content of her second periodical publishing venture, *New Era Magazine* (1916), Hopkins either received enough encouragement to resurrect the project she began at the *Colored American Magazine*, or she was simply convinced that the community still needed to be educated about success and uplift through literature. *New Era Magazine* is more outspoken about the necessity of blacks helping themselves and each other succeed, and of the magazine's own responsibility in contributing to the black community's success. In the "Editorial and Publisher's Announcements" for the February 1916 issue, Hopkins vows, "Under God we will use our every resource for the uplift of our people."[6] The most significant change in Hopkins's editorial vision is the global view of race relations and racial solidarity that she promoted in the magazine and that Freund had discouraged her from advocating while she was at the *Colored American Magazine*. The subtitle of *New Era Magazine* states that it is "An Illustrated Monthly Devoted to the World-Wide Interest of the Negro Race." In addition to printing articles about Liberia and Puerto Rico, Hopkins ran the section "Around the World of Color," which consisted of "General News Items of Interest to the Race from all Parts of the World."[7] She also began another biographical series, "Men of Vision," similar to "Famous Men of the Negro

Race." Nonetheless, despite Hopkins's lofty ambitions, the magazine lasted only two issues. It is not clear why, but it is easy to speculate that the masses of readers Hopkins was most intent on reaching out to, and speaking up for, simply could not afford to sustain the publication through subscriptions or charitable contributions.

Details about reactions from white readers are scarce. The closest evidence of a white reader's response to Hopkins's writing is a letter Cornelia Condict wrote to the editors of the *Colored American Magazine*. Condict criticized the magazine's serial novelists for writing stories that depict interracial love affairs: "The stories of these tragic mixed loves will not commend themselves to your white readers and will not elevate the colored readers" (399). Judging from this letter, and Hopkins's response, it is likely that many whites did not understand the nuances of Hopkins's critique of United States race relations and the American Dream. Although Condict does not mention Hopkins by name, Hopkins felt the need to defend her own work by explaining, "My stories are definitely planned to show the obstacles persistently placed in our paths by a dominant race to subjugate us spiritually. Marriage is made illegal between the races and yet the mulattoes increase. Thus the shadow of corruption [that] falls on the blacks and on the whites without whose aid the mulattoes would not exist. . . . I sing of the *wrongs* of a race that ignorance of their pitiful condition may be changed to intelligence and must awaken compassion in the hearts of the just."[8] This white reader did not understand Hopkins's strategy behind using interracial relationships to unveil the hypocrisy of whites that claim mulattoes are the byproduct of immoral blacks. Indeed, if whites that purported to support Hopkins's efforts (like John Freund) failed to recognize the value of using success literature to fight racist stereotypes while motivating blacks to succeed, then it is likely that the larger white community was even less sympathetic.

All African American leaders did not view the traditional gospel of success with the same degree of antagonism as Hopkins, however. In fact, Booker T. Washington worked assiduously to apply the traditional model to his own life, or rather to give others the perception that he had done so. Hopkins criticized the way Washington ignored American race prejudice as he appropriated the traditional paradigm to create his own prescription for African American success. Her outspoken position in favor of political agitation eventually forced her off the magazine staff. The world was not ready for Pauline Hopkins. She was one of the few black women to earn a living (modest though it was) as a magazine editor at a time when even few black men chose publishing as their sole profession.[9] Her contemporary black women writers were either not as prolific or committed to promoting African American success in all of their writings. For example, like Hopkins,

Alice Dunbar-Nelson produced literature in multiple genres, but unlike Hopkins, she did not tackle race head-on in her published fiction. Dunbar-Nelson reserved her political commentary for her nonfiction, whereas Hopkins presented declarative political statements in her nonfiction as well as her fiction. Indeed, Hopkins challenged black male leaders, liberal white male philanthropists, and white racists when doing so amounted to political and social suicide. Even though current scholarship applauds Hopkins's remarkable career achievements, there is a growing trend to characterize her actual tenure at the *Colored American Magazine* and a significant portion of her career as a failure.[10] Although Hopkins paid a price for being outspoken, labeling her a victim would diminish her fighting spirit, determination, and pure gumption. Hopkins was a renaissance woman whose stage and lecturing experience taught her how to draw in an audience, and whose periodical editorial experience taught her to give readers what they wanted to read without compromising her own principles. Her skill at interweaving multiple literary genres in one publication exemplifies her versatility, intellect, and creativity. In the prospectus for *Contending Forces*, Hopkins asked, "Of what use is fiction to the colored race at the present crisis in its history?"[11] Her work answers this question by illustrating how early twentieth-century black periodicals could not only entertain *and* educate an audience, but also serve as an effective vehicle for social and political protest. In this sense, Hopkins's writings and editorial decisions remind us not to minimize the power of popular success literature. The fact that Hopkins selected and published articles, short stories, and serialized fiction for a general black audience does not make her work any less valuable to African American literary history. Interestingly, once Hopkins became the editor of record in May 1903, she consistently used the title *literary* editor, not simply editor or any other variants, to designate her position with the magazine.

"Let the good work go on," Hopkins wrote in response to Condict's swipe at the *Colored American Magazine*'s fiction; "Opposition is the life of an enterprise; criticism tells you that you are doing something."[12] Hopkins utilized her editorial role to tailor a message to a black middle-class audience in a way that was accessible but not simplistic. She is an example of a writer who serviced the masses and held high expectations of her readers. Hopkins's solution to the race problem was to educate her entire community, whites and blacks, through success literature. In the spirit of Pauline Hopkins, scholars of African American literature and culture must endeavor to "Let the good work go on."

NOTES

Introduction

1. Pauline Hopkins, "The New York Subway," *The Voice of the Negro* (Dec. 1904): 605, 612.

2. Nell Irvin Painter, *Standing at Armageddon: The United States, 1877–1919* (New York: Norton, 1987), 37.

3. Paulette D. Kilmer, *The Fear of Sinking: The American Success Formula in the Gilded Age* (Knoxville: U of Tennessee P, 1996), 3.

4. Ibid., 51-52.

5. Richard Huber, *The American Idea of Success* (New York: McGraw-Hill, 1971), 1.

6. Ibid., 1.

7. Richard Weiss, *The American Myth of Success: From Horatio Alger to Norman Vincent Peale* (New York: Basic Books, 1969), 97-98.

8. Rex Burns, *Success in America: The Yeoman Dream and the Industrial Revolution* (Amherst: U of Massachusetts P, 1976), 1.

9. Kilmer, *Fear of Sinking*, 6.

10. Pauline Hopkins, *Contending Forces: A Romance Illustrative of Negro Life North and South* (New York: Oxford UP, 1988), 13-14.

11. Ann Allen Shockley, "Pauline Elizabeth Hopkins: A Biographical Excursion Into Obscurity," *Phylon* 33.1 (1972): 26.

12. Claudia Tate, "Pauline Hopkins: Our Literary Foremother," in *Conjuring: Black Women, Fiction, and Literary Tradition*, ed. Marjorie Pryse and Hortense J. Spillers (Bloomington: Indiana UP, 1985), 55-56.

13. Kate McCullough, "Slavery, Sexuality, and Genre: Pauline Hopkins and the Representation of Female Desire," in *The Unruly Voice: Rediscovering Pauline Elizabeth Hopkins*, ed. John Cullen Gruesser (Urbana: U of Illinois P, 1996), 22-23.

14. Gwendolyn Brooks, afterword to *Contending Forces*, by Pauline Hopkins (Carbondale: Southern Illinois UP, 1978), 409.

15. Ibid., 404-5.

16. Mary Helen Washington, *Invented Lives: Narratives of Black Women 1860–1960* (Garden City, N.Y.: Anchor Press, 1987), 79.

17. "Pauline Elizabeth Hopkins," in *Twentieth-Century Literary Criticism*, vol. 28, ed. Dennis Poupard (Detroit: Gale Research, 1988), 168.

18. Eric Foner, *A Short History of Reconstruction, 1863–1877* (New York: Harper & Row, 1990), 31.

19. Ibid., 252.

20. Frances Smith Foster and Richard Yarborough, "Literature of the Reconstruction to the New Negro Renaissance 1865–1919," in *The Norton Anthology of African American Literature*, ed. Henry Louis Gates Jr. and Nellie Y. McKay (New York: W. W. Norton, 1997), 468.

21. Henry Louis Gates Jr., "The Blackness of Blackness: a Critique of the Sign and the Signifying Monkey," in *Black Literature and Literary Theory*, ed. Henry Louis Gates Jr. (New York: Routledge, 1990), 285–86.

22. Henry Louis Gates Jr., *The Signifying Monkey: A Theory of African-American Literary Criticism* (New York: Oxford UP, 1988), 124.

23. Because I am utilizing Gates's literary theory of Signification, I follow his convention and capitalize the term Signify throughout this study. See Gates, *Signifying Monkey*, 45–51, for his explanation of the difference between the black "Signifyin(g)" and the standard English "signifying."

24. Scrapbook, Pauline E. Hopkins Collection, Fisk University. Folder 11.

25. Eileen Southern, ed., *African American Theater: Out of Bondage (1876) and Peculiar Sam; or, The Underground Railroad (1879)* (New York: Garland, 1994), xiii.

26. Leo Hamalian and James V. Hatch, ed., *The Roots of African American Drama: An Anthology of Early Plays, 1858–1938* (Detroit: Wayne State UP, 1991), 96.

27. Southern, *African American Theater*, xxiv.

28. Shockley, "Pauline Elizabeth Hopkins," 23.

29. Ann Allen Shockley, "Pauline Elizabeth Hopkins," in *Afro-American Women Writers 1746–1933: An Anthology and Critical Guide* (Boston: G. K. Hall, 1988), 292.

30. Richard Yarborough, introduction to *Contending Forces*, by Pauline Hopkins (New York: Oxford UP, 1988), xxviii.

31. Vernon Loggins, *The Negro Author: His Development in America to 1900* (New York: Columbia UP, 1931), 326; Hugh Gloster, *Negro Voices in American Fiction* (New York: Russell and Russell, 1965), 33.

32. Robert A. Bone, *The Negro Novel in America* (New Haven, Conn.: Yale UP, 1958), 26.

33. Washington, *Invented Lives*, xx.

34. Hazel Carby, *Reconstructing Womanhood: The Emergence of the Afro-American Woman Novelist.* (New York: Oxford UP, 1987), 122.

35. Ibid., 145.

36. Hazel Carby, introduction to *The Magazine Novels of Pauline Hopkins* (New York: Oxford UP, 1988), xxix.

37. Yarborough, introduction to *Contending Forces*, xxx, xxx–xxxi.

38. Claudia Tate, *Domestic Allegories of Political Desire: The Black Heroine's Text at the Turn of the Century* (New York: Oxford UP, 1992), 12.

Chapter 1

"To Aid in Everyway Possible in Uplifting the Colored People of America": Hopkins's Revisionary Definition of African American Success

1. Weiss, *American Myth of Success*, 3.

2. Cotton Mather, *A Christian at His Calling* . . . , in *The American Gospel of Success: Individualism and Beyond*, ed. Moses Rischin (Chicago: Quadrangle Books, 1965), 23.

3. Ibid., 25.

4. Burns, *Success in America*, 2.

5. Ibid., 3.

6. Ibid., 1.

7. Benjamin Franklin, *The Way to Wealth*, in Rischin, *American Gospel of Success*, 34, 35.

8. Weiss, *American Myth of Success*, 29.

9. Huber, *American Idea of Success*, 18–19.

10. John G. Cawelti, *Apostles of the Self-Made Man* (Chicago: U of Chicago P, 1965), 5.

11. Burns, *Success in America*, 167.

12. Kilmer, *Fear of Sinking*, 4.

13. Painter, *Standing at Armageddon*, 110.

14. Ibid., 176.

15. Weiss, *American Myth of Success*, 7.

16. Kilmer, *Fear of Sinking*, 3.

17. Cawelti, *Apostles of the Self-Made Man*, 47.

18. P. T. Barnum, *Art of Money-Getting*, in Rischin, *American Gospel of Success*, 65–66.

19. Weiss, *American Myth of Success*, 100–101.

20. John Sibley Butler, *Entrepreneurship and Self-Help* (New York: State U of New York P, 1991), 68.

21. Weiss, *American Myth of Success*, 116.

22. Michael Fultz, "'The Morning Cometh': African-American Periodicals, Education, and the Black Middle Class, 1900–1930," in *Print Culture in a Diverse America*, ed. James R. Danky and Wayne A. Wiegard (Urbana: U of Illinois P, 1998), 130.

23. Ibid., 143–44.

24. August Meier, *Negro Thought in America, 1880–1915: Radical Ideologies in the Age of Booker T. Washington* (Ann Arbor: U of Michigan P, 1963), 10.

25. Ibid., 15.

26. Ibid., 42.

27. Ibid., 23–24.

28. James Olney, "'I was Born': Slave Narratives, Their Status as Autobiography and as Literature," in *The Slave's Narrative*, ed. Charles T. Davis and Henry Louis Gates Jr. (Oxford: Oxford UP, 1985), 154.

29. Frederick Douglass, *Narrative of the Life of Frederick Douglass, an American Slave* (New York: Penguin, 1982), 148.

30. Ibid., 150.

31. A[bigail] Mott, compiler, *Biographical Sketches and Interesting Anecdotes of Persons of Color to which is Added, a Selection of Pieces of Poetry* (New York: Mahlon Day, 1837), n.p.

32. Ibid.

33. Ibid.

34. Henry Davenport Northrop, Joseph R. Gay, and I. Garland Penn, *The College of Life, or Practical Self-Educator* (n.p.: Horace C. Fry, 1900), iv.

35. Ibid.

36. Samuel Smiles, *Self-Help, with Illustrations of Character, Conduct, and Perseverance,* ed. Peter W. Sinnema (Oxford: Oxford UP, 2002), 3.

37. Ibid., 7.

38. Northrop, Gay, and Penn, *College of Life,* 111.

39. Ibid.

40. Ibid., 74.

41. Ibid., 75.

42. Ibid., 75, 77.

43. Pauline Hopkins, "Toussaint L'Overture," *Colored American Magazine* 2.1 (Nov. 1900): 9.

44. Northrop, Gay, and Penn, *College of Life,* 74; Hopkins, "Toussaint L'Overture," 11. Subsequent references to Hopkins's periodical publications will be made parenthetically within the text.

45. C. K. Doreski, "Inherited Rhetoric and Authentic History: Pauline Hopkins at the *Colored American Magazine*," in *The Unruly Voice: Rediscovering Pauline Elizabeth Hopkins,* ed. John Cullen Gruesser (Urbana: U of Illinois P, 1996), 72.

46. Ibid., 72, 73.

47. Smiles, *Self Help,* 18.

48. Sinnema, introduction to Smiles, *Self-Help,* xx.

49. Ibid., xxi.

50. Meier, *Negro Thought,* 24.

51. Thomas Carlyle, *Past and Present* (New York: AMS Press, 1974), 271–72.

52. Theodore Greene, *America's Heroes: The Changing Models of Success in American Magazines* (New York: Oxford UP, 1970), 141.

53. Ibid., 121.

54. Huber, *American Idea of Success,* 2.

55. Butler, *Entrepreneurship and Self-Help,* 72.

56. Greene, *America's Heroes,* 148–49.

57. Ibid., 151.

58. Doreski, "Inherited Rhetoric," 75.

59. Cawelti, *Apostles of the Self-Made Man,* 46.

60. Kilmer, *Fear of Sinking*, 10.

61. Greene, *America's Heroes*, 110.

62. Ibid., 119.

63. Ibid., 120.

64. Cawelti, *Apostles of the Self-Made Man*, 2.

Chapter 2

Furnace Blasts for the Tuskegee Wizard and the Talented Tenth: Hopkins and Her Contemporary Self-Made Men

1. W. E. B. Du Bois, "The Colored Magazine in America," *Crisis* 5.1 (Nov. 1912): 33.

2. William Stanley Braithwaite, "Negro America's First Magazine: How the Colored American Magazine Was Born," *Negro Digest* 6.2 (1947): 25.

3. See Jill Bergman, "'Everything we hoped she'd be': Contending Forces in Hopkins Scholarship," *African American Review* 38.2 (2004): 181-99.

4. See Hanna Wallinger, "Pauline E. Hopkins as Editor and Journalist: An African American Story of Success and Failure," in *Blue Pencils & Hidden Hands: Women Editing Periodicals, 1830–1910*, ed. Sharon M. Harris (Boston: Northeastern UP, 2004), 146-69. A variant of this article subsequently appears in Wallinger's *Pauline E. Hopkins: A Literary Biography* (Athens: U of Georgia P, 2005).

5. Phillipa Kafka, *The Great White Way: African-American Women Writers and American Success Mythologies* (New York: Garland Publishing, 1993), 15.

6. Meier, *Negro Thought*, 103, 106.

7. Ibid., 175.

8. See John Gruesser, "Taking Liberties: Pauline Hopkins's recasting of the Creole Rebellion," in *The Unruly Voice: Rediscovering Pauline Elizabeth Hopkins*, ed. John Gruesser (Urbana: U of Illinois P, 1996), 105; Julie Cary Nerad, "'So Strangely Interwoven': The Property of Inheritance, Race, and Sexual Morality in Pauline E. Hopkins's *Contending Forces*," *African American Review* 35. 3 (2001): 358; Erica Lorraine Griffin, "'The Living is (Not) Easy': Inverting African American Dreams Deferred in the Literary Careers of Pauline Elizabeth Hopkins, Jessie Redmon Fauset, and Dorothy West, 1900-1995," PhD diss., University of Georgia, 2002, 38.

9. Pauline E. Hopkins, *Contending Forces* (New York: Oxford UP, 1988), 288. Subsequent page numbers will be provided parenthetically in the text.

10. Carby, *Reconstructing Womanhood*, 139.

11. Meier, *Negro Thought*, 114.

12. Ibid., 112.

13. Ibid., 110, 113.

14. Ibid., 115.

15. W. E. B. Du Bois, "Industrial Education—Will it Solve the Negro Problem?" *Colored American Magazine* 7.5 (May 1904): 339.

16. Barbara McCaskill, "Anna Julia Cooper, Pauline Elizabeth Hopkins, and the African American Feminization of Du Bois's Discourse," in *The Souls of Black Folk One Hundred Years Later*, ed. Dolan Hubbard (Columbia: U of Missouri P, 2003), 71.

17. W. E. B. Du Bois, "Does Education Pay?" in *The Complete Published Works of W. E. B. Du Bois. Writings by W. E. B. Du Bois in Periodicals Edited By Others*, comp. and ed. Herbert Aptheker (Millwood, N.Y.: Krause-Thomson, 1982), 1–18. According to Lois Brown, Hopkins was "extremely active in the Colored National League and its affiliated circles." Brown, *Pauline Elizabeth Hopkins*, 167.

18. Booker T. Washington, "The Standard Printed Version of the Atlanta Exposition Address," in *The Booker T. Washington Papers*, ed. Louis R. Harlan and Raymond W. Smock, vol. 3 (Urbana: U of Illinois P, 1974), 583.

19. Washington, "Address," 585.

20. Ibid.

21. Brown, *Pauline Elizabeth Hopkins*, 410.

22. Abby Arthur Johnson and Ronald M. Johnson, "Away from Accommodation: Radical Editors and Protest Journalism, 1900–1910," *Journal of Negro History* 62.4 (1977): 325.

23. "Announcement," *Colored American Magazine* 1.1 (May 1900): n.p.

24. "Editorial and Publisher's Announcements," *Colored American Magazine* 1.1 (May 1900): 60.

25. "Editorial and Publisher's Announcements," 61.

26. Ibid., 61–62.

27. Ann Allen Shockley, "Pauline Elizabeth Hopkins: A Biographical Excursion Into Obscurity," *Phylon* 33.1 (1972): 24.

28. Hazel V. Carby, introduction to *The Magazine Novels of Pauline Hopkins*, by Pauline E. Hopkins (New York: Oxford UP, 1998), xxx–xxxi.

29. Hopkins to Trotter, April 16, 1905, in Hopkins Papers.

30. Meier, *Negro Thought*, 224–25.

31. Ibid., 236.

32. Meier, "Booker T. Washington," 87–88.

33. Hopkins to Trotter, April 16, 1905, in Hopkins Papers.

34. Booker T. Washington, "The Storm Before the Calm," *Colored American Magazine* 1.4 (Sept. 1900): 202.

35. "The Negro an Experiment," *Colored American Magazine* 1.4 (Sept. 1900): 263.

36. Verner Mitchell was the first scholar to note that Hopkins also used the pseudonym J. Shirley Shadrach, but he did not explain how he discovered Hopkins and Shadrach were one and the same. Verner Mitchell, "To Steal Away Home: Tracing Race, Slavery and Difference in Selected Writings of Thomas Jefferson, David Walker, William Wells Brown, Ralph W. Emerson and Pauline Hopkins," PhD diss., Rutgers University, 1995, 196.

37. "Editorial and Publisher's Announcements," *Colored American Magazine* 4.4 (Mar. 1902): 335.

38. Advertisement, *Colored American Magazine* 5.4 (Aug. 1902): n.p.; J. Shirley Shadrach, "Charles Winter Wood; or, From Bootblack to Professor," *Colored American Magazine* 5.5 (Sept. 1902): 345.

39. Washington, "The Storm," 202.

40. Ibid., 207.

41. Louis R. Harlan, *Booker T. Washington: The Making of a Black Leader, 1856–1901* (New York: Oxford UP, 1972), 243.

42. Booker T. Washington, "Negro Homes," *Colored American Magazine* 5.5 (Sept. 1902): 378.

43. Ibid., 379.

44. Carby, introduction to *The Magazine Novels of Pauline Hopkins*, xxxii.

45. Ibid., xxxv.

46. Walter Wallace to Booker T. Washington, August 6, 1901, in *The Booker T. Washington Papers* vol. 6, ed. Louis R. Harlan and Raymond W. Smock (Urbana: U of Illinois P, 1977), 184.

47. Ibid., 185.

48. Booker T. Washington to Francis Jackson Garrison, May 17, 1905, in *The Booker T. Washington Papers* vol. 8, ed. Louis R. Harlan and Raymond W. Smock (Urbana: U of Illinois P, 1979), 281.

49. Braithwaite, "Negro America's First Magazine," 26.

50. Austin N. Jenkins to Emmett Jay Scott, August 5, 1904, in *Washington Papers* vol. 8, 39–40.

51. W. E. B. Du Bois, "Debit and Credit," *Voice of the Negro* 2.1 (Jan. 1905): 277.

52. Oswald Garrison Villard to W. E. B. Du Bois, February 7, 1905, in *The Correspondence of W. E. B. Du Bois* vol. 1, *Selections, 1877–1934*, ed. Herbert Aptheker (Amherst: U of Massachusetts P, 1973), 97; Villard to Du Bois, March 13, 1905, in *Correspondence*, 97.

53. William Hayes Ward to Du Bois, February 18, 1905, in *Correspondence*, 96.

54. Du Bois to Ward, March 10, 1905, in *Correspondence*, 96.

55. Du Bois to William Monroe Trotter, March 15, 1905, in *Correspondence*, 97–98.

56. Trotter to Du Bois, March 18, 1905, in *Correspondence*, 98.

57. Du Bois to Villard, March 24, 1905, in *Correspondence*, 98–102.

58. Du Bois, "The Colored Magazine in America," 33.

59. Hopkins to Trotter, April 16, 1905, in Hopkins Papers; John C. Freund to Hopkins, April 7, 1904, in Hopkins Papers.

60. Ibid.

61. Freund to William H. Dupree, November 19, 1903, in Hopkins Papers.

62. Pauline E. Hopkins, "How a New York Newspaper man Entertained a Number of Colored Ladies and Gentlemen at Dinner," *Colored American Magazine* 7.3 (Mar. 1904): 158.

63. Hopkins to Trotter, April 16, 1905, in Hopkins Papers.

64. Ibid.

65. Freund to Dupree, January 27, 1904, in Hopkins Papers.

66. Hopkins to Trotter, April 16, 1905, in Hopkins Papers.

67. Freund to Hopkins, February 18, 1904, in Hopkins Papers.

68. Freund to Dupree, March 31, 1904, in Hopkins Papers.

69. Freund to Dupree, April 6, 1904, in Hopkins Papers.

70. "Publisher's Announcements," *Colored American Magazine* 7.4 (Apr. 1904): n.p.

71. Hopkins to Trotter, April 16, 1905, in Hopkins Papers.

72. Freund to Dupree, March 31, 1904, in Hopkins Papers.

73. Freund to Hopkins, April 11, 1904, in Hopkins Papers.

74. Hopkins to Trotter, April 16, 1905, in Hopkins Papers.

Chapter 3

"Mammon Leads Them On": Hopkins's Visionary Critique of the Gospel of Success

1. Carby, *Reconstructing Womanhood*, 144.

2. Tate, *Domestic Allegories*, 7.

3. Cawelti, *Apostles of the Self-Made Man*, 62.

4. Ibid.

5. Carby, introduction to *The Magazine Novels of Pauline Hopkins*, xxxv.

6. Carby, *Reconstructing Womanhood*, 145.

7. Kilmer, *Fear of Sinking*, 16.

8. Horatio Alger, *Ragged Dick* (New York: Collier-Macmillan, 1962). Subsequent references to this novel will be provided parenthetically in the text.

9. Cawelti, *Apostles of the Self-Made Man*, 108.

10. Carby, introduction to *The Magazine Novels of Pauline Hopkins*, xxxvi.

11. Brown, *Pauline Elizabeth Hopkins*, 113.

12. Cawelti, *Apostles of the Self-Made Man*, 117.

13. Pauline Hopkins, *Peculiar Sam; or, The Underground Railroad*, in *The Roots of African American Drama: An Anthology of Early Plays, 1858–1938*, ed. Leo Hamalian and James V. Hatch (Detroit: Wayne State UP, 1991) 104, 105. Subsequent page numbers will be provided parenthetically in the text.

14. Brown, *Pauline Elizabeth Hopkins*, 118, 119.

15. Weiss, *American Myth of Success*, 57.

16. Pauline Hopkins, "General Washington: A Christmas Story," in *Short Fiction by Black Women, 1900–1920*, ed. Elizabeth Ammons (New York: Oxford UP, 1991), 69. Subsequent page numbers will be provided parenthetically in the text.

17. Cawelti, *Apostles of the Self-Made Man*, 118.

18. Kilmer, *Fear of Sinking*, 11.

19. Horatio Alger, *Struggling Upward; or, Luke Larkin's Luck* (1890; New York: Penguin, 1986), 192. Subsequent page numbers will be provided parenthetically in the text.

20. Sarah A. Allen [Pauline Hopkins], "The Test of Manhood, A Christmas Story," in *Short Fiction by Black Women, 1900–1920*, ed. Elizabeth Ammons (New York:

Oxford UP, 1991), 205. Subsequent page numbers will be provided parenthetically in the text.

21. Cawelti, *Apostles of the Self-Made Man*, 118.

22. Pauline Hopkins, *Of One Blood; or, The Hidden Self*, in *The Magazine Novels of Pauline Hopkins*, ed. Henry Louis Gates Jr. (New York: Oxford UP, 1988), 443. Subsequent page numbers will be provided parenthetically in the text.

23. Debra Bernardi, "Narratives of Domestic Imperialism: The African-American Home in the Colored American Magazine and the Novels of Pauline Hopkins, 1900–1903," in *Separate Spheres No More: Gender Convergence in American Literature, 1830–1930*, ed. Monika M. Elbert (Tuscaloosa: U of Alabama P, 2000), 212.

24. John Gruesser, "Pauline Hopkins's Of One Blood: Creating an Afrocentric Fantasy for a Black Middle Class Audience," in *Modes of the Fantastic: Selected Essays from the Twelfth International Conference on the Fantastic in the Arts*, ed. Robert A. Latham and Robert A. Collins (Westport, Conn.: Greenwood Press, 1995), 74.

25. Ibid., 76.

26. Ibid.

27. Hanna Wallinger, "Voyage into the Heart of Africa: Pauline Hopkins and *Of One Blood*," in *Black Imagination and the Middle Passage*, ed. Maria Diedrich, Henry Louis Gates Jr., and Carl Pedersen (New York: Oxford UP, 1999), 211.

Chapter 4

"In the Lives of These Women are Seen Signs of Progress": Hopkins's Race Woman and the Gospel of Success

1. "Report of the Woman's Era Club for 1899," *The National Association Notes* 3.10 (Apr. 1900): 1.

2. Ibid.

3. Ibid.

4. For more on the contested NACW elections, see Sharon Harley, "Mary Church Terrell: Genteel Militant," in *Black Leaders of the Nineteenth Century*, ed. Leon Litwack and August Meier (Urbana: U of Illinois P, 1988), 307–21 and Mary Church Terrell, *A Colored Woman in a White World* (New York: Hall, 1996).

5. "Mrs. Ruffin's Attacks" is handwritten by an unknown person on the front page of *The National Notes* issue containing the Woman's Era Club's resolutions. A microfilm copy of this issue is located at Rutgers University.

6. Rodger Streitmatter, *Raising Her Voice: African-American Women Journalists Who Changed History* (Lexington: UP of Kentucky, 1994), 64.

7. Siobhan Somerville, "Passing through the Closet in Pauline E. Hopkins's *Contending Forces*," *American Literature* 69.1 (Mar. 1997): 155.

8. Yarborough, introduction to *Contending Forces* , xl.

9. Ibid., xlvi.

10. Thomas Cassidy, "Contending Contexts: Pauline Hopkins's *Contending Forces*," *African American Review* 32.4 (1998): 662.

11. Wallinger, *Pauline E. Hopkins*, 106.

12. Cassidy, "Contending Contexts," 661.

13. Tate, *Domestic Allegories*, 6.

14. Josephine St. Pierre Ruffin, "Greeting," *Woman's Era* 24 (Mar. 1894): 8.

15. Francesca Sawaya, *Modern Women, Modern Work: Domesticity, Professionalism, and American Writing, 1890–1950* (Philadelphia: U of Pennsylvania P, 2004), 40.

16. McCullough, "Slavery, Sexuality, and Genre," 24.

17. Karol Kelley, *Models for the Multitudes: Social Values in the American Popular Novel, 1850–1920* (New York: Greenwood, 1987), 30.

18. Ibid., xvii, xviii.

19. Barbara Welter, "The Cult of True Womanhood: 1820–1860," *American Quarterly* 18.2 (1966): 152; Jeffrey Louis Decker, *Made in America: Self-Styled Success from Horatio Alger to Oprah Winfrey* (Minneapolis: U of Minnesota P, 1997), 27.

20. Welter, "Cult of True Womanhood," 152.

21. Elaine Ognibene, "Women to Women: The Rhetoric of Success for Women, 1860–1920," PhD diss., Rensselear Polytechnic Institute, 1979, 26–27.

22. Josie Briggs Hall, *Hall's Moral and Mental Capsule for the Economic and Domestic Life of the Negro, as a Solution of the Race Problem* (Dallas: Rev. R. S. Jenkins, 1905), 1.

23. Ibid., 5.

24. Josephine St. Pierre Ruffin, "Address of Josephine St. P. Ruffin, President of Conference," *Woman's Era* (Aug. 1895): 14.

25. Pauline Hopkins, "Famous Women of the Negro Race: Higher Education of Colored Women in White Schools and Colleges," *Colored American Magazine*, 5.6 (Oct. 1902): 445. Subsequent references to the "Famous Women" series will be provided parenthetically within the text.

26. Washington, *Invented Lives*, 76.

27. Decker, *Made in America*, 17.

28. Ibid., 17.

29. Deborah White, *Too Heavy a Load: Black Women in Defense of Themselves 1894–1994* (New York: Norton, 1999), 27–28.

30. Decker, *Made in America*, 18.

31. Somerville, "Passing through the Closet," 154.

32. Cassidy, "Contending Contexts," 666.

33. Wallinger, *Pauline Elizabeth Hopkins*, 105.

34. Tate, *Domestic Allegories*, 164.

35. Ruffin, "Address," 14.

36. Tate, *Domestic Allegories*, 164.

37. Ognibene, "Women to Women," 159.

38. Carby, *Reconstructing Womanhood*, 131.

39. Sarah A. Allen [Pauline Hopkins], *Hagar's Daughter: A Story of Southern Caste Prejudice*, in *The Magazine Novels of Pauline Hopkins*, ed. Henry Louis Gates Jr. (New York: Oxford UP, 1988), 9. Subsequent page numbers will be provided parenthetically in the text.

40. Elizabeth Ammons, "Afterword: Winona, Bakhtin, and Hopkins in the Twenty-First Century," in *The Unruly Voice: Rediscovering Pauline Elizabeth Hopkins*, ed. John Cullen Gruesser (Urbana: U of Illinois P, 1996), 214.

41. Jerome Hamilton Buckley, *Season of Youth: The Bildungsroman from Dickens to Golding* (Cambridge, Mass.: Harvard U P, 1974), vii–viii.

42. Ibid., viii.

43. Martin Japtok, *Growing up Ethnic: Nationalism and the Bildungsroman in African American and Jewish American Fiction* (Iowa City: U of Iowa P, 2005), 21.

44. Ammons, "Afterword," 216.

45. Buckley, *Season of Youth*, 17.

46. Pauline Hopkins, *Winona: A Tale of Negro Life in the South and Southwest*, in *The Magazine Novels of Pauline Hopkins*, ed. Henry Louis Gates Jr. (New York: Oxford UP, 1988), 291. Subsequent page numbers will be provided parenthetically in the text.

47. Buckley, *Season of Youth*, 17.

48. Japtok, *Growing up Ethnic*, 26.

49. Buckley, *Season of Youth*, 17–18.

50. Ibid., 18.

Conclusion

"Let the Good Work Go On"

1. Hopkins to Trotter, April 16, 1905, in Hopkins Papers.

2. "Read What They Say of the *Colored American Magazine*," *Colored American Magazine* 7.4 (Apr. 1904): 395.

3. Alberta Moore Smith, "Comment," Colored American Magazine 3.6 (Oct. 1901): 479.

4. "Editorial and Publisher's Announcements," *Colored American Magazine* 1.5 (Oct. 1900): 333.

5. Advertisement, *Colored American Magazine* 3.3 (July 1901): n.p.

6. "Editorial and Publisher's Announcements," *New Era Magazine* (Feb. 1916): 60.

7. "Around the World of Color," *New Era Magazine* (Feb. 1916): 54.

8. Pauline Hopkins, response to Cornelia A. Condict, *Colored American Magazine* 6.5 (Mar. 1903): 399.

9. Carrie A. Bannister edited the *Future State* (Kansas City, Mo.) with Ernest D. Lynwood in the 1890s. See Penelope L. Bullock, *The Afro-American Periodical Press* (Baton Rouge: Louisiana State UP, 1981), 90.

10. See Wallinger, "Pauline E. Hopkins as Editor and Journalist," 147.

11. "Prospectus of the New Romance of Colored Life, *Contending Forces*," *Colored American Magazine* 1.4 (Sept. 1900): n.p.

12. Pauline E. Hopkins, Response to Cornelia A. Condict, *Colored American Magazine* 6.5 (Mar. 1903): 400. For Condict's original letter to the editor, see *Colored American Magazine* 6.5 (Mar. 1903): 398–99.

BIBLIOGRAPHY

Advertisement. *Colored American Magazine* 3.3 (July 1901): n.p.

Alger, Horatio. *Helen Ford*. 1866. Philadelphia: Polyglot Press, 2002.

———. *Mark, the Match Boy*. 1869. New York: Collier-Macmillan, 1962.

———. *Ragged Dick*. 1868. New York: Collier-Macmillan, 1962.

———. *Struggling Upward; or, Luke Larkin's Luck*. 1890. New York: Penguin, 1986.

Allen, Sarah A. [Pauline Hopkins]. *Hagar's Daughter: A Story of Southern Caste Prejudice*. 1901-2. In Hopkins, *Magazine Novels*, 1-284.

———. "Latest Phases of the Race Problem in America." *Colored American Magazine* 6.4 (Feb. 1903): 244-51.

———. "Mr. M. Hamilton Hodges." *Colored American Magazine* 7.3 (Mar. 1904): 167-68.

———. "The Test of Manhood, A Christmas Story." 1902. In Ammons, *Short Fiction*, 205-17.

Ammons, Elizabeth. Afterword. In Gruesser, *The Unruly Voice*, 211-19.

———, comp. *Short Fiction by Black Women, 1900-1920*. New York: Oxford University Press, 1991.

"Announcement." *Colored American Magazine* 1.1 (May 1900): n.p.

"Announcement for 1902." *Colored American Magazine* 4.5 (Apr. 1902): n.p.

Aptheker, Herbert, ed. *The Correspondence of W. E. B. Du Bois*. Vol. 1. Selections, 1877-1934. Amherst: University of Massachusetts Press, 1973.

"Around the World of Color." *New Era Magazine* (Feb. 1916): 54-59.

Barnum, P. T. *The Art of Money-Getting, or Hints and Helps How to Make a Fortune*. 1882. In Rischin, *The American Gospel of Success*, 47-66.

Bergman, Jill. "'Everything we hoped she'd be': Contending Forces in Hopkins Scholarship," *African American Review* 38.2 (2004): 181-99.

Bernardi, Debra. "Narratives of Domestic Imperialism: The African-American Home in the Colored American Magazine and the Novels of Pauline Hopkins, 1900-1903." In *Separate Spheres No More: Gender Convergence in American Literature, 1830-1930*. Ed. Monika M. Elbert. Tuscaloosa: University of Alabama Press, 2000. 203-24.

Bone, Robert A. *The Negro Novel in America*. New Haven, Conn.: Yale University Press, 1958.

Braithwaite, William Stanley. "Negro America's First Magazine." *Negro Digest* 6.2 (1947): 21-26.

Brooks, Gwendolyn. Afterword. *Contending Forces: A Romance Illustrative of Negro Life North and South.* By Pauline Hopkins. 1900. Carbondale: Southern Illinois University Press, 1978. 403-9.

Brown, Hallie Q. *Homespun Heroines and Other Women of Distinction.* New York: Oxford University Press, 1988.

Brown, Lois. *Pauline Elizabeth Hopkins: Black Daughter of the Revolution.* Chapel Hill: University of North Carolina Press, 2008.

Buckley, Jerome Hamilton. *Season of Youth: The Bildungsroman from Dickens to Golding.* Cambridge, Mass.: Harvard University Press, 1974.

Bullock, Penelope L. *The Afro-American Periodical Press, 1838-1909.* Baton Rouge: Louisiana State University Press, 1981.

Burns, Rex. *Success in America: The Yeoman Dream and the Industrial Revolution.* Amherst: University of Massachusetts Press, 1976.

Butler, John Sibley. *Entrepreneurship and Self-Help Among Black Americans: A Reconsideration of Race and Economics.* New York: State University of New York Press, 1991.

Carby, Hazel. Introduction to *The Magazine Novels of Pauline Hopkins,* by Pauline Hopkins. New York: Oxford University Press, 1988. xxix-l.

——. *Reconstructing Womanhood: The Emergence of the Afro-American Woman Novelist.* New York: Oxford University Press, 1987.

Carlyle, Thomas. *Past and Present.* New York: AMS Press, 1974.

Cassidy, Thomas. "Contending Contexts: Pauline Hopkins's *Contending Forces.*" *African American Review* 32.4 (1998): 661-72.

Cawelti, John G. *Apostles of the Self-Made Man.* Chicago: University of Chicago Press, 1965.

Condict, Cornelia A. Letter to the Editor. *Colored American Magazine* 6.5 (Mar. 1903): 398-99.

Daniel, Walter C. *Black Journals of the United States: Historical Guide to the World's Periodicals and Newspapers.* Westport, Conn.: Greenwood Press, 1982.

Decker, Jeffrey Louis. *Made In America: Self-Styled Success from Horatio Alger to Oprah Winfrey.* Minneapolis: University of Minnesota Press, 1997.

Doreski, C. K. "Inherited Rhetoric and Authentic History: Pauline Hopkins at the Colored American Magazine." In Gruesser, *The Unruly Voice,* 71-97.

Douglass, Frederick. *Narrative of the Life of Frederick Douglass, an American Slave.* 1845. New York: Penguin, 1982.

Du Bois, W. E. B. "The Colored Magazine in America." *The Crisis* (Nov. 1912): 33-35.

——. "Does Education Pay?" In *The Complete Published Works of W. E. B. Du Bois. Writings by W. E. B. Du Bois in Periodicals Edited By Others.* Comp. and ed. Herbert Aptheker. Millwood, N.Y.: Krause-Thomson, 1982.

——. "Industrial Education—Will it Solve the Negro Problem." *Colored American Magazine* 7.5 (May 1904): 333-39.

——. Letter to Oswald Garrison Villard. March 24, 1905. In Aptheker, 98–102.

——. Letter to William Hayes Ward. March 10, 1905. In Aptheker, 96.

——. Letter to William Monroe Trotter. March 15,1905. In Aptheker, 97–98.

Dworkin, Ira. Introduction. *Daughter of the Revolution: The Major Nonfiction Works of Pauline E. Hopkins.* Ed. Ira Dworkin. New Brunswick, N.J.: Rutgers University Press, 2007. xix–xliv.

"Editorial and Publisher's Announcements." *Colored American Magazine* 1.1 (May 1900): 60–64.

"Editorial and Publisher's Announcements." *Colored American Magazine* 1.5 (Oct. 1900): 333.

"Editorial and Publisher's Announcements." *New Era Magazine* (Feb. 1916): 60–62.

Elliot, R. S. "The Story of Our Magazine." *Colored American Magazine* (May 1901): 43–77.

Foner, Eric. *A Short History of Reconstruction, 1863–1877.* New York: Harper & Row, 1990.

Foster, Frances Smith, and Richard Yarborough. "Literature of the Reconstruction to the New Negro Renaissance 1865–1919." In *The Norton Anthology of African American Literature.* Ed. Henry Louis Gates Jr. and Nellie Y. McKay. New York: W. W. Norton, 1997. 461–72.

Franklin, Benjamin. *The Way to Wealth.* 1757. In Rischin, *The American Gospel of Success,* 33–38.

Freund, John C. Letter to William H. Dupree. November 19, 1903. Pauline Hopkins Collection. Fisk University, Franklin Library Special Collections, Nashville.

——. Letter to William H. Dupree. January 27, 1904. Pauline Hopkins Collection. Fisk University, Franklin Library Special Collections, Nashville.

——. Letter to William H. Dupree. March 31, 1904. Pauline Hopkins Collection. Fisk University, Franklin Library Special Collections, Nashville.

——. Letter to William H. Dupree. April 6, 1904. Pauline Hopkins Collection. Fisk University, Franklin Library Special Collections, Nashville.

——. Letter to Pauline E. Hopkins. February 18, 1904. Pauline Hopkins Collection. Fisk University, Franklin Library Special Collections, Nashville.

——. Letter to Pauline E. Hopkins. April 11, 1904. Pauline Hopkins Collection. Fisk University, Franklin Library Special Collections, Nashville.

Fultz, Michael. "'The Morning Cometh': African-American Periodicals, Education, and the Black Middle Class, 1900–1930." In *Print Culture in a Diverse America.* Ed. James R. Danky and Wayne A. Wiegard. Urbana: University of Illinois Press, 1998. 129–48.

Gaines, Kevin. "Black Americans' Racial Uplift Ideology as 'Civilizing Mission': Pauline E. Hopkins on Race and Imperialism." In *Cultures of United States Imperialism.* Ed. Amy E. Kaplan and Donald E. Pease. Durham, N.C.: Duke University Press, 1993. 433–55.

Gates, Henry Louis, Jr. "The Blackness of Blackness: A Critique of the Sign and the Signifying Monkey." In *Black Literature and Literary Theory.* Ed. Henry Louis Gates Jr. New York: Routledge, 1990. 285–321.

——. *The Signifying Monkey: A Theory of African-American Literary Criticism.* New York: Oxford University Press, 1988.

Gloster, Hugh. *Negro Voices in American Fiction.* 1948. New York: Russell and Russell, 1965.

Greene, Theodore P. *America's Heroes: The Changing Models of Success in American Magazines.* New York: Oxford University Press, 1970.

Griffin, Erica Lorraine. "'The Living is (Not) Easy': Inverting African American Dreams Deferred in the Literary Careers of Pauline Elizabeth Hopkins, Jessie Redmon Fauset, and Dorothy West, 1900–1995." PhD diss., University of Georgia, 2002.

Gruesser, John. "Pauline Hopkins's Of One Blood: Creating an Afrocentric Fantasy for a Black Middle Class Audience." In *Modes of the Fantastic: Selected Essays from the Twelfth International Conference on the Fantastic in the Arts.* Ed. Robert A. Latham and Robert A. Collins. Westport, Conn.: Greenwood Press, 1995. 74–83.

——. "Taking Liberties: Pauline Hopkins's Recasting of the Creole Rebellion." In Gruesser, *The Unruly Voice,* 98–118.

——, ed. *The Unruly Voice: Rediscovering Pauline Elizabeth Hopkins.* Urbana: University of Illinois Press, 1996.

Hall, Josie Briggs. *Hall's Moral and Mental Capsule for the Economic and Domestic Life of the Negro, as a Solution of the Race Problem.* Dallas: Rev. R. S. Jenkins, 1905.

Hamalian, Leo, and James V. Hatch, eds. *The Roots of African American Drama: An Anthology of Early Plays, 1858–1938.* Detroit: Wayne State University Press, 1991.

Harlan, Louis R. *Booker T. Washington: The Making of a Black Leader, 1856–1901.* New York: Oxford University Press, 1972.

Harley, Sharon. "Mary Church Terrell: Genteel Militant." In *Black Leaders of the Nineteenth Century.* Ed. Leon Litwack and August Meier. Urbana: University of Illinois Press, 1988. 307–21.

Hopkins, Pauline E. *Contending Forces: A Romance Illustrative of Negro Life North and South.* 1900. Ed. Henry Louis Gates Jr. New York: Oxford University Press, 1988.

——. "Famous Men of the Negro Race: Booker T. Washington." *Colored American Magazine* 3.6 (Oct. 1901): 436–41.

——. "Famous Men of the Negro Race: Charles Lenox Remond." *Colored American Magazine* 3.1 (May 1901): 34–39.

——. "Famous Men of the Negro Race: Edwin Garrison Walker." *Colored American Magazine* 2.5 (Mar. 1901): 358–66.

——. "Famous Men of the Negro Race: John Mercer Langston." *Colored American Magazine* 3.3 (July 1901): 177–84.

——. "Famous Men of the Negro Race: Lewis Hayden." *Colored American Magazine* 2.6 (Apr. 1901): 473–77.

——. "Famous Men of the Negro Race: Robert Browne [sic] Elliott." *Colored American Magazine* 2.4 (Feb. 1901): 294–301.

——. "Famous Men of the Negro Race: Robert Morris." *Colored American Magazine* 3.5 (Sept. 1901): 337–42.

——. "Famous Men of the Negro Race: Sargeant [sic] William H. Carney." *Colored American Magazine* 3.2 (June 1901): 84-89.

——. "Famous Men of the Negro Race: Senator Blanche K. Bruce." *Colored American Magazine* 3.4 (Aug. 1901): 257-61.

——. "Famous Women of the Negro Race: Artists." *Colored American Magazine* 5.5 (Sept. 1902): 362-67.

——. "Famous Women of the Negro Race: Club Life Among Colored Women." *Colored American Magazine* 5.4 (Aug. 1902): 273-77.

——. "Famous Women of the Negro Race: Educators." *Colored American Magazine* 5.1 (May 1902): 41-46.

——. "Famous Women of the Negro Race: Educators (Continued)." *Colored American Magazine* 5.2 (June 1902): 125-30.

——. "Famous Women of the Negro Race: Educators (Concluded)." *Colored American Magazine* 5.3 (July 1902): 206-13.

——. "Famous Women of the Negro Race: Harriet Tubman." *Colored American Magazine* 4.3 (Jan.-Feb. 1902): 210-23.

——. "Famous Women of the Negro Race: Higher Education of Colored Women in White Schools and Colleges." *Colored American Magazine* 5.6 (Oct. 1902): 445-50.

——. "Famous Women of the Negro Race: Phenomenal Vocalists." *Colored American Magazine* 4.1 (Nov. 1901): 45-53.

——. "Famous Women of the Negro Race: Sojourner Truth." *Colored American Magazine* 4.2 (Dec. 1901): 124-32.

——. "Famous Women of the Negro Race: Some Literary Workers." *Colored American Magazine* 4.4 (Mar. 1902): 274-80.

——. "Famous Women of the Negro Race: Some Literary Workers (Concluded)." *Colored American Magazine* 4.5 (Apr. 1902): 366-71.

——. "General Washington: A Christmas Story." 1900. In Ammons, *Short Fiction*, 69-82.

——. "Heroes and Heroines in Black. I. Neil Johnson, Americas Woodfolk, et al." *Colored American Magazine* 6.3 (Jan. 1903): 206-11.

——. "Hon. Frederick Douglass." *Colored American Magazine* 2.2 (Dec. 1900): 121-32.

——. "How a New York Newspaper Man Entertained a Number of Colored Ladies and Gentlemen at Dinner [. . .]." *Colored American Magazine* 7.3 (Mar. 1904): 151-60.

——. Letter to W[illiam] M[onroe] Trotter. April 16, 1905. Pauline Hopkins Collection. Fisk University, Franklin Library Special Collections, Nashville.

——. *The Magazine Novels of Pauline Hopkins*. Ed. Henry Louis Gates Jr. New York: Oxford University Press, 1988.

——. "Men of Vision: No.1. Mark Rene Demortie." *New Era Magazine* (Feb. 1916): 35-39.

——. "Men of Vision: No. 2. Rev. Leonard Andrew Grimes." *New Era Magazine* (Mar. 1916): 99-105.

———. "Munroe Rogers." *Colored American Magazine* 6.1 (Nov. 1902): 20–26.

———. "The New York Subway." *The Voice of the Negro* (Dec. 1904): 605–12.

———. *Of One Blood; or, The Hidden Self.* 1902–3. In Hopkins, *Magazine Novels,* 439–621.

———. Pauline Hopkins Collection [papers]. Fisk University, Franklin Library Special Collections, Nashville.

———. *Peculiar Sam; or, The Underground Railroad.* 1879. In Hamalian and Hatch, 100–123.

———. Response to Cornelia A. Condict. *Colored American Magazine* 6.5 (Mar. 1903): 399–400.

———. "Toussaint L'Overture [sic]." *Colored American Magazine* 2.1 (Nov. 1900): 9–24.

———. "William Wells Brown." *Colored American Magazine* 2.3 (Jan. 1901): 232–36.

———. *Winona: A Tale of Negro Life in the South and Southwest.* 1902. In Hopkins, *Magazine Novels,* 285–437.

Huber, Richard. *The American Idea of Success.* New York: McGraw-Hill, 1971.

Japtok, Martin. *Growing Up Ethnic: Nationalism and the Bildungsroman in African American and Jewish American Fiction.* Iowa City: University of Iowa Press, 2005.

Jenkins, Austin N. "Austin N. Jenkins to Emmett Jay Scott." August 5, 1904. In *The Booker T. Washington Papers.* Ed. Louis R. Harlan and Raymond W. Smock. Vol. 8. Urbana: University of Illinois Press, 1979. 39–40.

Johnson, Abby Arthur, and Ronald Maberry Johnson. "Away From Accommodation: Radical Editors and Protest Journalism, 1900–1910." *Journal of Negro History* 62.4 (1977): 325–38.

Kafka, Phillipa. *The Great White Way: African-American Women Writers and American Success Mythologies.* New York: Garland Publishers, 1993.

Kelley, Karol. *Models for the Multitudes: Social Values in the American Popular Novel, 1850–1920.* New York: Greenwood Press, 1987.

Kilmer, Paulette D. *The Fear of Sinking: The American Success Formula in the Gilded Age.* Knoxville: University of Tennessee Press, 1996.

Knight, Alisha R. "'All Things Work Together For Good': Pauline Hopkins's Race Woman and the Gospel of Success." In *Loopholes and Retreats: African American Writing and the Nineteenth Century.* Ed. John Cullen Gruesser and Hanna Wallinger. Munster, Ger.: Lit-Verlag, 2008.

———. "Furnace Blasts for the Tuskegee Wizard: Revisiting Pauline Elizabeth Hopkins, Booker T. Washington, and the *Colored American Magazine.*" *American Periodicals* 17.1 (2007): 41–64.

Loggins, Vernon. *The Negro Author: His Development in America to 1900.* New York: Columbia University Press, 1931.

Lohof, Bruce A. "Helen Ford: Horatio Alger Jr.'s Book for Girls." *Journal of Popular Culture* 17.4 (1984): 97–105.

Mather, Cotton. *A Christian at His Calling; Two Brief Discourses. One Directing a Christian in His General Calling; Another Directing Him in His Personal.* 1701. In Rischin, *The American Gospel of Success,* 23–30.

McCaskill, Barbara. "Anna Julia Cooper, Pauline Elizabeth Hopkins, and the African American Feminization of Du Bois's Discourse." In *The Souls of Black Folk One Hundred Years Later*. Ed. Dolan Hubbard. Columbia: University of Missouri Press, 2003. 70–84.

McCullough, Kate. "Slavery, Sexuality, and Genre: Pauline Hopkins and the Representation of Female Desire." In Gruesser, *The Unruly Voice*, 21–49.

Meier, August. "Booker T. Washington and the Negro Press, with Special Reference to the Colored American Magazine." *Journal of Negro History* 38 (1953): 67–90.

——. *Negro Thought in America, 1880–1915: Radical Ideologies in the Age of Booker T. Washington*. Ann Arbor: University of Michigan Press, 1963.

Mitchell, Verner. "To Steal Away Home: Tracing Race, Slavery, and Difference in Selected Writings of Thomas Jefferson, David Walker, William Wells Brown, Ralph Waldo Emerson, and Pauline Elizabeth Hopkins." PhD diss., Rutgers University, 1995.

Mott, A[bigail], comp. *Biographical Sketches and Interesting Anecdotes of Persons of Color to which is Added, a Selection of Pieces of Poetry*. New York: Mahlon Day, 1837.

"The Negro: An Experiment." *Colored American Magazine* 1.4 (Sept. 1900): 262–63.

Nerad, Julie Cary. "'So Strangely Interwoven': The Property of Inheritance, Race, and Sexual Morality in Pauline E. Hopkins's *Contending Forces*." *African American Review* 35.3 (2001): 357–73.

Northrop, Henry Davenport, Joseph R. Gay, and I. Garland Penn. *The College of Life, or Practical Self-Educator*. n.p.: Horace Fry, 1900.

Ognibene, Elaine R. "Women to Women: The Rhetoric of Success for Women, 1860–1920." PhD diss., Rensselaer Polytechnic Institute, 1979.

Olney, James. "'I Was Born': Slave Narratives, their Status as Autobiography and as Literature." In *The Slave's Narrative*. Ed. Charles T. Davis and Henry Louis Gates Jr. Oxford: Oxford University Press, 1985. 148–75.

Painter, Nell Irvin. *Standing at Armageddon: The United States, 1877–1919*. New York: Norton, 1987.

"Pauline Hopkins." *Colored American Magazine* 2.3 (Jan. 1901): 218–19.

"Pauline Elizabeth Hopkins." In *Twentieth-Century Literary Criticism*. Vol. 28. Ed. Dennis Poupard. Detroit: Gale Research, 1988. 168–77.

Porter, Dorothy B. "Hopkins, Pauline Elizabeth." In *Dictionary of American Negro Biography*. Ed. Rayford W. Logan and Michael R. Winston. New York: W. W. Norton, 1982. 325–26.

Pratt, Annis. *Archetypal Patterns in Women's Fiction*. Bloomington: Indiana University Press, 1981.

"Prospectus of the New Romance of Colored Life, *Contending Forces*." *Colored American Magazine* 1.4 (Sept. 1900): n.p.

"Publishers' Announcements." *Colored American Magazine* 7.4 (Apr. 1904): n.p.

"Read What They Say of The *Colored American Magazine*." *Colored American Magazine* 2.5 (Mar. 1901): 395.

"Report of the Woman's Era Club for 1899." *The National Association Notes* 3.10 (Apr. 1900): 1–2.

Rischin, Moses, ed. *The American Gospel of Success: Individualism and Beyond*. Chicago: Quadrangle Books, 1965.

Rose Bibliography Project. *Analytical Guide and Indexes to The Colored American Magazine 1900–1909*. Westport, Conn.: Greenwood Press, 1974.

Ruffin, Josephine St. Pierre. "Address of Josephine St. P. Ruffin, President of Conference." *Woman's Era* (Aug. 1895): 13–15. *Emory Woman Writers Resource Project at the Lewis H. Beck Center*. Emory University. June 12, 2007. http://chaucer.library.emory.edu/wwrp

——. "Greeting." *Woman's Era* (Mar. 24, 1894): 8. *Emory Woman Writers Resource Project at the Lewis H. Beck Center*. Emory University. June 12, 2007. http://chaucer.library.emory.edu/wwrp

Sawaya, Francesca. *Modern Women, Modern Work: Domesticity, Professionalism, and American Writing, 1890–1950*. Philadelphia: University of Pennsylvania Press, 2004.

Shadrach, J. Shirley [Pauline Hopkins]. "Charles Winter Wood; or, From Bootblack to Professor." *Colored American Magazine* 5.5 (Sept. 1902): 345–48.

——. "Rev. John Henry Dorsey." *Colored American Magazine* 5.6 (Oct. 1902): 411–17.

——. "William Pickens, Yale University." *Colored American Magazine* 6.7 (July 1903): 517–21.

Shockley, Ann Allen. "Pauline Elizabeth Hopkins." In *Afro-American Women Writers 1746–1933: An Anthology and Critical Guide*. Boston: G. K. Hall, 1988. 289–94.

——. "Pauline Elizabeth Hopkins: A Biographical Excursion Into Obscurity." *Phylon* 33.1 (Spring 1972): 22–26.

Sinnema, Peter W. Introduction to *Self-Help*, by Samuel Smiles. Oxford: Oxford University Press, 2002. vii–xxviii.

Smiles, Samuel. *Self-Help, with Illustrations of Character, Conduct, and Perseverance*. Ed. Peter W. Sinnema. Oxford: Oxford University Press, 2002.

Smith, Alberta Moore. "Comment." *Colored American Magazine* 3.6 (Oct. 1901): 479.

Somerville, Siobhan. "Passing through the Closet in Pauline E. Hopkins's *Contending Forces*." *American Literature* 69.1 (1997): 139–66.

Southern, Eileen, ed. *African American Theater: Out of Bondage* (1876) *and Peculiar Sam; or, The Underground Railroad* (1879). New York: Garland, 1994.

Streitmatter, Rodger. *Raising Her Voice: African-American Women Journalists Who Changed History*. Lexington: University Press of Kentucky, 1994.

Tate, Claudia. *Domestic Allegories of Political Desire: The Black Heroine's Text at the Turn of the Century*. New York: Oxford University Press, 1992.

——. "Pauline Hopkins: Our Literary Foremother." In *Conjuring: Black Women, Fiction, and Literary Tradition*. Ed. Marjorie Pryse and Hortense J. Spillers. Bloomington: Indiana University Press, 1985. 53–66.

Terrell, Mary Church. *A Colored Woman in a White World*. New York: Hall, 1996.

Villard, Oswald Garrison. Letter to W. E. B. Du Bois. February 7, 1905. In Aptheker, 97.

——. Letter to W. E. B. Du Bois. March 13, 1905. In Aptheker, 97.

Wallace, Walter "From Walter N. Wallace." Letter to Booker T. Washington. August 6, 1901. In *The Booker T. Washington Papers*. Ed. Louis R. Harlan and Raymond W. Smock. Vol. 6. Urbana: University of Illinois Press, 1977. 184-85.

Wallinger, Hanna. *Pauline E. Hopkins: A Literary Biography*. Athens: University of Georgia Press, 2005.

——. "Voyage into the Heart of Africa: Pauline Hopkins and *Of One Blood*." In *Black Imagination and the Middle Passage*. Ed. Maria Diedrich, Henry Louis Gates Jr., and Carl Pedersen. New York: Oxford University Press, 1999. 203-14.

Walther, Malin LaVon. "Works By and About Pauline Hopkins." In Gruesser, *The Unruly Voice*, 221-30.

Ward, William Hayes. Letter to W. E. B. Du Bois. February 18, 1905. In Aptheker, 96.

Washington, Booker T. "The Storm Before the Calm." *Colored American Magazine* 1.4 (Sept. 1900): 199-213.

——. "Negro Homes." *Colored American Magazine* 5.5 (Sept. 1902): 378-79.

——. "The Standard Printed Version of the Atlanta Exposition Address." In *The Booker T. Washington Papers*. Ed. Louis R. Harlan and Raymond W. Smock. Vol. 3. Urbana: University of Illinois Press, 1974. 583-87.

——. "To Francis Jackson Garrison." May 17, 1905. In *The Booker T. Washington Papers*. Ed. Louis R. Harlan and Raymond W. Smock. Vol. 8. Urbana: University of Illinois Press, 1979. 279-83.

——. *Up From Slavery*. 1901. Oxford: Oxford University Press, 1995.

Washington, Mary Helen. *Invented Lives: Narratives of Black Women 1860-1960*. Garden City, N.Y.: Anchor Press, 1987.

Weiss, Richard. *The American Myth of Success: From Horatio Alger to Norman Vincent Peale*. New York: Basic Books, 1969.

Welter, Barbara. "The Cult of True Womanhood: 1820-1860." *American Quarterly* 18.2 (1966): 151-74.

White, Deborah Gray. *Too Heavy a Load: Black Women in Defense of Themselves, 1894-1994*. New York: W. W. Norton, 1999.

Yarborough, Richard. Introduction to *Contending Forces*, by Pauline Hopkins. New York: Oxford University Press, 1988. xxvii-xlviii.

INDEX

Pauline Hopkins and the American Dream was designed and typeset on a Macintosh 10.6 computer system using InDesign CS5 software. The body text is set in 10.5/13 Goudy Old Style and display type is set in Goudy Old Style Bold. This book was designed and typeset by Barbara Karwhite and manufactured by Thomson-Shore, Inc.